T0196104

MACAT

An Analysis of

Jared Diamond's

Guns, Germs, and Steel
The Fate of Human Societies

Riley Quinn

ROUTLEDGE

Published by Macat International Ltd
24:13 Coda Centre, 189 Munster Road, London SW6 6AW.

Distributed exclusively by Routledge
2 Park Square, Milton Park, Abingdon, Oxon OX14 4RN
711 Third Avenue, New York, NY 10017, USA

Routledge is an imprint of the Taylor & Francis Group, an informa business

www.macat.com
info@macat.com

Cataloguing in Publication Data
A catalogue record for this book is available from the British Library.
Library of Congress Cataloguing-in-Publication Data is available upon request.
Cover illustration: A. Richard Allen

ISBN 978-1-912302-02-4 (hardback)
ISBN 978-1-912127-97-9 (paperback)
ISBN 978-1-912128-27-3 (e-book)

Notice
The information in this book is designed to orientate readers of the work under analysis,
to elucidate and contextualise its key ideas and themes, and to aid in the development
of critical thinking skills. It is not meant to be used, nor should it be used, as a
substitute for original thinking or in place of original writing or research. References and
notes are provided for informational purposes and their presence does not constitute
endorsement of the information or opinions therein. This book is presented solely for
educational purposes. It is sold on the understanding that the publisher is not engaged
to provide any scholarly advice. The publisher has made every effort to ensure that
this book is accurate and up-to-date, but makes no warranties or representations with
regard to the completeness or reliability of the information it contains. The information
and the opinions provided herein are not guaranteed or warranted to produce particular
results and may not be suitable for students of every ability. The publisher shall not be
liable for any loss, damage or disruption arising from any errors or omissions, or from
the use of this book, including, but not limited to, special, incidental, consequential or
other damages caused, or alleged to have been caused, directly or indirectly, by the
information contained within.

CONTENTS

THE MACAT LIBRARY

The Macat Library is a series of unique academic explorations of seminal works in the humanities and social sciences – books and papers that have had a significant and widely recognised impact on their disciplines. It has been created to serve as much more than just a summary of what lies between the covers of a great book. It illuminates and explores the influences on, ideas of, and impact of that book. Our goal is to offer a learning resource that encourages critical thinking and fosters a better, deeper understanding of important ideas.

Each publication is divided into three Sections: Influences, Ideas, and Impact. Each Section has four Modules. These explore every important facet of the work, and the responses to it.

This Section-Module structure makes a Macat Library book easy to use, but it has another important feature. Because each Macat book is written to the same format, it is possible (and encouraged!) to cross-reference multiple Macat books along the same lines of inquiry or research. This allows the reader to open up interesting interdisciplinary pathways.

To further aid your reading, lists of glossary terms and people mentioned are included at the end of this book (these are indicated by an asterisk [*] throughout) – as well as a list of works cited.

Macat has worked with the University of Cambridge to identify the elements of critical thinking and understand the ways in which six different skills combine to enable effective thinking.
Three allow us to fully understand a problem; three more give us the tools to solve it. Together, these six skills make up the **PACIER** model of critical thinking. They are:

ANALYSIS – understanding how an argument is built
EVALUATION – exploring the strengths and weaknesses of an argument
INTERPRETATION – understanding issues of meaning

CREATIVE THINKING – coming up with new ideas and fresh connections
PROBLEM-SOLVING – producing strong solutions
REASONING – creating strong arguments

To find out more, visit **WWW.MACAT.COM.**

CRITICAL THINKING AND *GUNS, GERMS AND STEEL*

Primary critical thinking skill: REASONING
Secondary critical thinking skill: INTERPRETATION

In his 1997 work *Guns, Germs and Steel*, Jared Diamond marshals evidence from five continents and across 13,000 years of human history in an attempt to answer the question of why that history unfolded so differently in various parts of the globe. His results offer new explanations for why the unequal divisions of power and wealth so familiar to us today came into existence – and have persisted.

Balancing materials drawn from a vast range of sources, addressing core problems that have fascinated historians, anthropologists, biologists and geographers alike – and blending his analysis to create a compelling narrative that became an international best-seller and reached a broad general market – required a mastery of the critical thinking skill of reasoning that few other scholars can rival. Diamond's reasoning skills allow him to persuade his readers of the value of his interdisciplinary approach and produce well-structured arguments that keep them turning pages even as he refocuses his analysis from one disparate example to another.

Diamond adds to that a spectacular ability to grasp the meaning of the available evidence produced by scholars in those widely different disciplines – making *Guns, Germs and Steel* equally valuable as an exercise in high-level interpretation.

ABOUT THE AUTHOR OF THE ORIGINAL WORK

Born in Boston in the United States in 1937, **Jared M. Diamond** studies human history using a wide-ranging approach that draws on biology, anthropology, ecology, and geography. He first trained as a biochemist at Harvard University and as a physiologist at Cambridge University, but became interested in ecology when he visited New Guinea in 1964. He then developed an interest in environmental history, and is now professor of geography at the University of California, Los Angeles, as well as an environmental activist and popular writer. He won the prestigious Pulitzer Prize for his 1997 work *Guns, Germs, and Steel.*

ABOUT THE AUTHOR OF THE ANALYSIS

Riley Quinn holds master's degrees in politics and international relations from both LSE and the University of Oxford.

ABOUT MACAT

GREAT WORKS FOR CRITICAL THINKING

Macat is focused on making the ideas of the world's great thinkers accessible and comprehensible to everybody, everywhere, in ways that promote the development of enhanced critical thinking skills.

It works with leading academics from the world's top universities to produce new analyses that focus on the ideas and the impact of the most influential works ever written across a wide variety of academic disciplines. Each of the works that sit at the heart of its growing library is an enduring example of great thinking. But by setting them in context – and looking at the influences that shaped their authors, as well as the responses they provoked – Macat encourages readers to look at these classics and game-changers with fresh eyes. Readers learn to think, engage and challenge their ideas, rather than simply accepting them.

WAYS IN TO THE TEXT

KEY POINTS

- Jared Diamond's 1997 book *Guns, Germs, and Steel: The Fates of Human Societies* won the highly respected Pulitzer Prize* for General Nonfiction in 1998.

- In *Guns, Germs, and Steel*, Diamond argues that geographic factors have a significant influence on history.

- Diamond's book compares historical cases with very large spans of time and distance between them—that is, it uses the comparative method* of historical analysis on a very large scale.

Who Was Jared Diamond?

Jared Diamond, the author of *Guns, Germs, and Steel: The Fates of Human Societies*, was born in Boston in 1937. He is an American evolutionary biologist, anthropologist, ecologist, and historian. His father was a pediatrician—a doctor specializing in children—and his mother was a concert pianist and a teacher of languages; thanks, in part, to his mother's influence, he can speak 12 languages.

His interest in so many fields follows his training in biochemistry (the chemical processes that occur inside living things) at Harvard University in the US, and his later training in physiology (anatomical structures) in England, at Cambridge University. He finished his studies in 1965 and, after a stint at Harvard, became professor of physiology at the medical school of the University of California, Los Angeles (UCLA). At this point, his career as an ecologist was born.

He developed a passion for ornithology—the study of birds—and began visiting the South Pacific island of New Guinea regularly. Although these trips were initially to study the island's birds, he also became attached to the people. A chance meeting with a local politician called Yali* sparked Diamond's interest in the development of human societies. In *Guns, Germs, and Steel*, Diamond applies his previous training to the analysis of human societies.

At the age of 65, Diamond completely abandoned his initial career in medical science and physiology, and devoted himself entirely to environmental history and evolutionary biology. He is now a professor of geography at UCLA, where he pursues his two other main interests: environmental activism that focuses on conservation efforts in New Guinea, and writing books about history aimed at general readers.

What Does *Guns, Germs, and Steel* Say?

Guns, Germs, and Steel is Jared Diamond's attempt to answer a question he was asked by Yali, the politician he met on one of his trips to New Guinea. "Why is it," Yali asked, "that you white people developed so much cargo [that is, material goods] and brought it to New Guinea, but we black people had little cargo of our own?"[1] In effect, Yali wanted Diamond to give him an account of a phenomenon called "uneven development"*—the disparities in technology, wealth, standards of living, freedom, and other key factors, all around the world. Why, in short, are some countries "developed" and others "developing"?

Diamond's answer to this question focused on long-term causes; he examined, in fact, a 13,000-year span of history to argue that key moments that contributed to today's development imbalance took place between the fifteenth and nineteenth centuries, when Europeans conquered much of the world. But European conquest is only what Diamond calls the "proximate" cause (meaning the closest, most obvious factor driving the change). He is not interested in proximate causes, wanting to find the "ultimate" cause—the underlying, long-term factor—that gave rise to the proximate cause.

The answer, he finds, is to do with the invention of agriculture. When people give up hunting and gathering in favor of agriculture, he argues, they are no longer focused on subsistence—that is, meeting the needs of their immediate survival—by following resources such as seasonal rain and migrating animals. They are necessarily less mobile. And eventually, towns and cities are formed. Every member of a hunter-gatherer* community spends many hours looking for food. But in agricultural communities, only some work in food production; others work as leaders, scribes, warriors, smiths, scientists, and so on. And organization like this is required for the development of things such as writing and technology.

Diamond does not leave the argument there, however. Why is it, he asks, that some societies become agricultural in the first place? And to answer *that*, he points to geography. Plants and animals that can be easily domesticated* are unevenly distributed, he points out; the majority are in southwest and southeast Eurasia. And the arrangement of Eurasia itself along an east–west axis, as opposed to a north–south axis, makes the exchange of plants and ideas in this region easier.

Because Eurasia contains long stretches of similar land, societies throughout history have been able to share solutions to common problems. Beyond this region, however, where there were fewer plants and animals that could be domesticated, hunter-gatherers would not have been able to change their lifestyle even if the idea had occurred to them. Random geographical factors and the unequal distribution of resources, then, set the stage for modern international inequality.

When *Guns, Germs, and Steel* was published in 1997, it became an international phenomenon. It was awarded both the prestigious

Pulitzer Prize in General Nonfiction and the Phi Beta Kappa Award in Science, awarded to significant books in science. It has been translated into 36 languages and is a fixture on undergraduate reading lists around the world. This is, in part, because of its application of the comparative method of historical analysis: it is an attempt to "do" history as a science.

Why Does *Guns, Germs, and Steel* Matter?

The book also provides an introduction to the "comparative method" of history—the application of scientific reasoning to questions about historical causes. A g the comparative method aims to look at *similar* cases that produced *different* outcomes and *different* cases that produced *similar* outcomes. From this, important further questions arise: What was different in the two similar cases? What was similar in the different cases? This helps establish *causation*—that is, it explains which factor caused which outcome.

The comparative method is a powerful tool. It can be used in nearly every discipline that looks at causes. For example, it is often used in the study of politics to establish conclusions. Students can look at countries that succeed in developing, and others that remain underdeveloped.* They can look at policy choices made in the past, and compare them to argue why they resulted in different outcomes.

Comparison and evidence are two key concepts in developing critical thinking. Critical thinking looks beyond surface-level ideas, and uses a rational system to understand what is really going on. A non-scientific approach to human history would have had little chance of identifying the causes of development 13,000 years ago.

Students can also develop critical thinking skills by looking at Diamond's critics. Even though Diamond is a critical historian who attempts to undermine the assumptions of others, he has some assumptions of his own. For example, some critics have suggested that Diamond's work is not as scientific as he says it is, and that he makes assumptions that are "culturally bound" (that is, he works with the assumption that certain Western ideas about what societies "should do" have a universal application).

NOTES

1   Jared Diamond, *Guns, Germs, and Steel: The Fates of Human Societies* (New York: W. W. Norton & Company, 1999), 14.

SECTION 1
INFLUENCES

MODULE 1
THE AUTHOR AND THE HISTORICAL CONTEXT

KEY POINTS

- *Guns, Germs, and Steel* presents a scientific study of inequality, using data from the past 13,000 years.

- Diamond's experience of life on the island of New Guinea inspired him to explore why some countries were underdeveloped* compared with others.

- The end of the Cold War* between the West and the former Soviet Union and the rise of globalization* (the interconnected nature of the world's economies, peoples, and cultures) put these questions at the forefront of debate.

Why Read This Text?

Jared Diamond's book *Guns, Germs, and Steel* examines the ultimate causes behind broad patterns of history. His argument is that, over the last 13,000 years of human history, contrasting paths of development between different peoples are the result of environmental differences between continents rather than biological differences between peoples. The title of the book refers to the proximate causes (that is, the immediate answers) to the question of why the European conquest of the Americas proceeded as it did. Diamond believes we cannot stop our inquiry there, however, and follows the chains of causation that show how each of these proximate factors result from an ultimate cause—environmental differences between continents and the rise of food production.

He attempts a scientific approach to human history, piecing

> ** 66 ** How big is the gap between rich and poor and
> what is happening to it? Very roughly and briefly: the
> difference in income per head between the richest
> industrial nation, say Switzerland, and the poorest non-
> industrial country, Mozambique, is about 400 to 1. ** 99 **
>
> David Landes, *The Wealth and Poverty of Nations*

together ideas from diverse disciplines to establish a broad theory
about human development. He uses a comparative approach*
borrowed from biology to test his theories relating to "broad patterns
that occur across space and time that do not require experimental
manipulation."[1] In other words, he compares historical circumstances
divided by great geographical and chronological distances in order to
discover why outcomes of different kinds occurred.

He conducts his search for answers by tracing the "chains of
causation" beyond the factors that obviously affected the accumulation
of power and wealth—guns, germs, and steel. According to his thesis,
the ultimate causes that explain the different outcomes in human
development are environmental differences between continents, and
favorable or unfavorable conditions for the rise and spread of food
production.

Guns, Germs, and Steel demonstrates that it is possible to take a
broad and bold interdisciplinary approach to answering history's most
important questions.

Author's Life

Jared Diamond was born in Boston in 1937. His mother was a
musician and amateur linguist, his father the associate chief of staff of
the Children's Hospital at Harvard Medical School and a specialist in
blood diseases. Diamond majored in biochemistry at Harvard College;
throughout his schooling he expected to become a physician like his

father. In the last undergraduate year, however, he shifted his focus to biological research and studied as a postgraduate at Cambridge University in England for a PhD in physiology.

World War II* was an important factor in shaping Diamond's world-view. He traveled through Europe after his PhD and learned how people's experiences of the war had shaped their lives. "Depending on whether they are English, German, Finnish, or Yugoslav," Diamond said, "born in 1937, I immediately knew whether their lives had suffered some major disruption" such as losing parents or homes. His conclusion was that "it was just an accident of whether they had been born in London, Berlin, Helsinki, or Zagreb."[2] This concern with the ways in which our opportunities are shaped by our circumstances would come to the fore later in his career.

His focus shifted away from medical laboratory research in 1964 when he traveled to the Pacific island of New Guinea, where he developed a passion for ecology and biology. As he became increasingly interested in the wildlife and people of New Guinea, his career also changed. His earlier focus on medicine and anatomy expanded to history, geography, ecology, biology, and anthropology. Although Diamond never had any formal training in these fields he has published many papers since the 1970s, influenced by his 26 trips to New Guinea for field research.

Author's Background

Diamond wrote *Guns, Germs, and Steel* in the mid-1990s. For much of his life—from 1945 to 1989—world politics had been shaped by the Cold War and the antagonistic relationship between the United States and the Soviet Union.

In the aftermath of the Cold War, though, new relationships— between developed and developing countries, and between developing countries themselves—took on a new importance. "We live in stirring times," opens the United Nations'* 1990 *Human Development Report*;

political systems and economic structures, it continues, "are beginning to change in countries where democratic forces had long been suppressed."[3] In other words, connections between the developed and the developing world were increasing in number and importance—and questions arose as to why some nations remained undeveloped, and what could be done about it.

The American economist and historian David Landes,* whose book *The Wealth and Poverty of Nations* was published at about the same time as Diamond's, suggests why it was timely and important to account for this uneven development.* "The old division of the world into two power blocs, East and West, has subsided," he wrote, and in the aftermath of ideological stand-offs and looming nuclear war "the big challenge and threat is the gap in wealth and health that separates rich and poor."[4] If the problems of development and uneven development are to be addressed, then their ultimate causes need to be discovered. Both Diamond and Landes aimed to uncover the root causes.

NOTES

1   Christopher Miller, "Review of *Guns, Germs, and Steel: The Fate of Human Societies*, by Jared Diamond," *Economic Botany* 56, no. 2 (2002): 209.

2   Jared Diamond, "About Me," accessed May 30, 2015, http://www.jareddiamond.org/Jared_Diamond/About_Me.html.

3   Mahbub ul-Haq, ed., *Human Development Report 1990* (New York: Oxford University Press, 1990), iii.

4   David Landes, *The Wealth and Poverty of Nations: Why Some Are So Rich and Some Are So Poor* (New York: W. W. Norton & Company, 1998), xx.

MODULE 2
ACADEMIC CONTEXT

KEY POINTS

- The study of "man–land"* geography emphasizes the relationship between humanity and its environment.

- In the work of such scientists as the influential English naturalist Charles Darwin* (who famously described the principles of evolution in 1859) and the French historian Fernand Braudel* (a key figure in the Annales school* of history), the scientific method has been used to explain the relationship between underlying factors and results.

- The scientific method crosses over to other, related, social science disciplines such as processual archaeology* (which seeks to establish "laws" of human behavior to explain archaeological evidence) and environmental sociology (which seeks to understand social behavior in the context of the environment).

The Work in its Context

Jared Diamond's *Guns, Germs, and Steel* is an interdisciplinary work—it draws on the aims and methods of different academic disciplines. Although it is relevant to the study of history, politics, and physical sciences, it is particularly relevant to the study of geography.

According to the American geographer William D. Pattison,* there are four main traditions of geography: the spatial tradition, the area studies tradition, the earth science tradition, and the "man–land" tradition.[1] "Spatial" geography compares the "distance, form, direction, and position" of different things and focuses mainly on maps and the physical features of the land. "Area studies" is interested in "the nature

> ❝ New [processual] archaeology stressed theory formation, model building, and hypothesis testing in the search for general laws of human behavior. Perhaps its most important contribution was its focus on culture process rather than culture history. ❞
>
> Timothy K. Earle and Robert W. Preucel, "Processual Archaeology and the Radical Critique"

of places, their character and their differentiation" beyond their physical features; it usually focuses on describing socio-political differences, rather than analyzing their origins. "Earth science," such as the study of geology, applies physics and chemistry to understanding the physical world.[2] Of these, Diamond's book is in the "man–land" tradition.

"Man-land" approaches to geography, which often include aspects of sociology (the study of the history and functioning of human society), look at the interaction between places (geography) and people (sociology), and how this shapes events throughout time (history). Structuralism,* an approach to the study of human culture founded on the idea that human actions are shaped by their place in a larger system,[3] is particularly important to man–land studies. In Diamond's case, the important factors of the larger system are environmental.

Overview of the Field

In his deeply influential book *On the Origin of Species* (1859), the English naturalist Charles Darwin explained the relationship between creatures and plants and their environments. His theory of natural selection* showed how environmental conditions shaped particular characteristics through "the preservation of favorable variations and the rejection of injurious variations."[4] This idea is relevant to our topic in its understanding of the role of nature. Darwin's idea that, over time, nature makes "winners" and "losers" was applied (or, rather, *misapplied*) to account for variations among human societies.

The American geographer Ellsworth Huntington's* book *Civilization and Climate* (1915) is an example of such a misapplication. In it, he argues that there is a relationship between climate and society. "We realize that a dense and progressive population cannot live in the far North or in deserts simply because the difficulty of getting a living grinds men down and keeps them isolated."[5] Huntington's insight is to connect a particular culture to the needs of living in a certain place. His argument becomes problematic, however, when he emphasizes the role of race, comparing "Teutons" (German speakers) and "negroes" (people of African descent). Huntington believes that "as the plum differs from the apple not only in outward form and color, but in inward flavor, so the negro seems to differ from the white man ... in the workings of the mind."[6] This idea—that non-white people are naturally inferior and that their civilizations are destined to be inferior—was used for centuries to justify the expansion of European empires.

The French historian Fernand Braudel and the Annales school with which he was associated, named after the journal of historical inquiry that he co-edited, took a much broader view. This approach examines the *longue durée**—the long-term and invisible factors that shape events and whose change is so slow as to be invisible (the slow depletion of a forest, for example, that changes the nature of a local economy, and that in turn could give rise to a new government).

For Braudel, the "general conditions of human life" are not the edicts of kings, but the earth's peninsulas, seas, and mountains; non-human factors, in other words, shape human outcomes. Braudel's seminal book, *The Mediterranean World in the Age of Philip II* (1949), begins with an analysis of the *physical* environment of the Mediterranean world in the 1500s. Although Braudel's period of focus in the book is short—1550 to 1600—the matter of his study comes from "evidence, images, and landscapes dating from other periods … [combined] across time and space."[7]

Academic Influences

Diamond was deeply influenced by the idea that the physical environment created the structures from which outcomes emerged. In his book, he applies it to archaeology. The American anthropologist Julien Steward,* who subscribes to the school of processual archaeology and its scientific rather than historical approach to the field of archaeology, writes that "All men eat, but this is an organic and not a cultural fact … What and how different groups of men eat is a cultural fact explainable only by culture history and environmental factors."[8]

Processual archaeology is not only interested in "organic" facts but "cultural facts." An organic fact might be evidence that people ate wheat; a "cultural fact" might be what it *meant* to them, and what we can learn from that about ancient agriculture in general. This approach sees archaeology not as a window into a static moment in time but as a series of clues from which we can both deduce facts about ancient peoples and draw conclusions about human behavior in general.

As well as processual archaeology, Diamond was influenced by the field of environmental sociology. Developed by the American sociologists Riley Dunlap* and William Catton,* it "involves recognition of the fact that physical environments can influence (and in turn be influenced by) human societies and behavior."[9] This was a new turn in sociology, which until this point had been interested, for the most part, in the ways in which groups of people relate to one another. Introducing the environment as a new variable brought "man–land" geography and sociology together.

NOTES

1   William D. Pattison, "The Four Traditions of Geography," *Journal of Geography* 63, no. 5 (1964): 211–16.

2   Pattison, "The Four Traditions of Geography," 211–16.

3   Pattison, "The Four Traditions of Geography."

4   Charles Darwin, *On the Origin of Species* (Oxford: Oxford University Press, 2008), 64.

5   Ellsworth Huntington, *Civilization and Climate* (New Haven, CT: Yale University Press, 1915), 2.

6   Huntington, *Civilization and Climate*, 16.

7   Fernand Braudel, *The Mediterranean World in the Age of Philip II: Volume I* (London: University of California Press, 1995), 23.

8   Julien Steward, *Theory of Culture Change: The Methodology of Multilinear Evolution* (Chicago: University of Illinois Press, 1972), 8.

9   Riley Dunlap and William Catton, "Environmental Sociology," *Annual Review of Sociology* 5 (1979): 244.

MODULE 3
THE PROBLEM

KEY POINTS

- Academics asked why there was inequality between states, given that people are the same around the world (no group of people is inherently cleverer or more inventive).

- World-systems theory* attributed underdevelopment* to oppression; many other theories of uneven development* argued it was due to divergences between Europe and the rest of the world in the seventeenth century.

- Diamond looked much further into the past. He argued that the explanations centered on the seventeenth century were not explaining the real causes, which were to be found in prehistory.

Core Question

As we have seen, Jared Diamond frames the core question of *Guns, Germs, and Steel* in terms of a question put to him by a New Guinean named Yali,* a friend of Diamond's and a local politician. "Why is it," he asked, "that you white people developed so much cargo [material goods] and brought it to New Guinea, but we black people had little cargo of our own?"[1] Yali was asking why some parts of the world experienced rapid economic development and other parts did not, a question that became extremely important in the latter half of the twentieth century as the process of globalization*—the process by which the world becomes more closely integrated culturally, economically, and politically—became increasingly prevalent.

Given the close and increasing contact between cultures with different levels of economic development, it was increasingly

> **❝** Oriental civilizations struck Europeans as monumental and grand. Much of the apparent grandeur was a compound of imposing works of civil engineering and luxury for the court circles. Mechanical engineering lagged. The standard of living of the mass of the people languished ... Overall, these societies were not rich in the sense of high average real incomes, the dimension in which Europe was to surpass them. **❞**
>
> Eric Jones, *The European Miracle*

important to account for these differences. Diamond, a scientist to the core, was determined not to frame this question in terms of simple and somewhat offensive causes related to technology, intelligence, and culture. Instead he tried a more rigorous methodological approach. For this reason, Diamond's question is not "Why is there inequality?" but rather "What is the real source of all the factors that have led to inequality?" Posing this question led Diamond's investigation back in time 13,000 years.

The Participants

Other thinkers approaching this question tended to place the moment of divergence that resulted in European dominance in the sixteenth and seventeenth centuries.

Immanuel Wallerstein's* "world systems theory" was one of the key explanations of different levels of development. The theory rested on the differences between "core" and "periphery" nations in terms of who performed the labor required for certain nations to prosper. "In the late fifteenth and early sixteenth century," Wallerstein argued, "there came into existence what we may call a European world-economy."[2] By this, he means that labor came to be divided between European core nations and non-European periphery nations. "In the geo-economically peripheral areas of the emerging world-economy," he continued, "there were two principal activities: mines [and] agriculture." Resources from these mines and plantations were forcibly transported back to the core nations.[3]

Wallerstein locates the origins of this situation in the capitalist* ideology of Western Europe, according to which those who perform labor do their work with resources and tools owned by those who profit. So capitalism requires the existence of owning classes and working classes.

The British Australian economic historian Eric Jones's* seminal book *The European Miracle*, written in 1981, argues (in line with the earlier arguments of Fernand Braudel* and Wallerstein) that the moment in which it was decided that Europe would dominate the world occurred in the sixteenth century, when the continent "underwent those political, technological, and geographical upheavals which were to make it the birthplace of the industrial world."[4] These upheavals arose from a multitude of factors, from Europe's geography to its style of political organization.

Europe's rapid advances in technology from the sixteenth century onward were unique because, as Jones argued, "cultural connections and the competitive nature of the states system encouraged continual borrowing and 'stimulus diffusion' which meant that if a problem were solved in one country it was assumed it could be solved in another."[5] In other words, European countries were separate enough to compete but close enough for solutions to common problems to spread rapidly. This analysis of the conjunctions of people and place is typical of Jones's approach.

The Contemporary Debate

In *Guns, Germs, and Steel*, Diamond writes that he sets his own argument against those based, like Ellsworth Huntington's,* on racial pseudo-science—non-scientific arguments that adopt the language of science. "Probably the commonest explanation" for the different levels of development between Europe and the rest of the world, he writes, "involves implicitly or explicitly assuming biological differences among peoples."[6] Diamond does not necessarily argue against academic arguments that involve this implicit prejudice; indeed such arguments became discredited generations ago. He argues, rather, against broad cultural assumptions outside academia.

His book is a far more popular work than others written in the second half of the twentieth century. Unlike most academic works, it is written mostly in non-academic language and without citation. In fact, one of the criticisms of Diamond's book was that it failed almost entirely to take part in the debates of the time in geography, history, or archaeology.[7]

Who, then, is Diamond really challenging? He is confronting those arguments that trace inequality to a "moment" of divergence in the fifteenth and sixteenth centuries, when Europe leapt ahead in its population, food production, and technology. This, though, only answers part of the question. Diamond believes nobody has looked adequately at the underlying cause of divergence—nor the underlying causes of those underlying causes.

NOTES

1   Jared Diamond, *Guns, Germs, and Steel: The Fates of Human Societies* (New York: W. W. Norton & Company, 1999), 14.

2   Immanuel Wallerstein, *The Modern World System I: Capitalist Agriculture and the Origins of the European World Economy in the Sixteenth Century* (London: University of California Press, 2011), 15.

3   Wallerstein, *The Modern World System*, 100.

4   Eric Jones, *The European Miracle: Environments, Economies, and Geopolitics in the History of Europe and Asia* (Cambridge: Cambridge University Press 2003), 225.

5   Jones, *The European Miracle*, 45.

6   Diamond, *Guns, Germs, and Steel*, 18–19.

7   Richard York and Philip Mancus, "Diamond in the Rough: Reflections on *Guns, Germs, and Steel,*" *Research in Human Ecology* 14, no. 2 (2007): 159.

MODULE 4
THE AUTHOR'S CONTRIBUTION

KEY POINTS

- Diamond believes the roots of modern inequality are to be found in geography, which is the only thing that differentiated societies 13,000 years ago (before the invention of agriculture).

- Diamond's approach combined many different fields—geology, archaeology, sociology, and others—using natural experiments* (that is, the opportunity to compare groups of people living in different conditions to understand why they arrived at different outcomes).

- Diamond broadened the scale and scope of a question about human development that had been asked throughout the twentieth century.

Author's Aims

Jared Diamond summarized his key argument in *Guns, Germs, and Steel* in one sentence:"History followed different courses for different people because of differences among peoples' environments, not because of biological differences among peoples themselves."[1]

The main focus of Diamond's book, however, is not merely the rejection of "biological" theories of difference. He wants, rather, to search beyond explanations that provide "parts of the puzzle, but … provide only pieces of the needed broad synthesis that has been missing."[2] This is a "structural"* exploration of history—it focuses on the ways in which human behavior outcomes are shaped by factors outside people's control.

Diamond intended his work to explore "ultimate" rather than

> ❝ A technique that frequently proves fruitful in …
> historical disciplines is the so-called natural experiment
> or the comparative method. This approach consists of
> comparing … different systems that are similar in many
> respects but differ with respect to the factors whose
> influence one wishes to study. ❞
>
> Jared Diamond and James Robinson, *Natural Experiments of History*

"proximate" causes of Western dominance—that is, the foundational causes, not the immediate causes. To do this, he had to trace the fundamental factors that enabled this dominance. Diamond believed that if an analysis should find that Western dominance occurred due to technological superiority, then that analysis was not thorough enough. If being ahead in technology allowed the West to dominate, then what was the reason for this technological superiority? This question cannot be answered without an analysis that considers some 13,000 years of history and accounts for the beginnings of civilization—far earlier than the fifteenth century, when consequences with ancient origins were felt in the colonized world.

Approach

Jared Diamond takes a scientific approach to the study of history in *Guns, Germs, and Steel*, and uses archaeological and environmental evidence from the physical world to build his argument. His book begins with an examination of "human history on all the continents, for millions of years, from our origins as a species until 13,000 years ago";[3] his aim is to present "human history as a science, on a par with acknowledged historical sciences such as astronomy, geology, and evolutionary biology."[4]

Since Diamond does not have a laboratory where he can run

controlled experiments on different populations, he takes advantage of what he calls "natural experiments" by comparing two populations that differ in a certain way—a population that develops agriculture and another that does not, for example.[5] As a result, some of Diamond's comparisons are drawn on a large scale. They look at continent-sized regions that differ in their plant and animal populations, or their climate, or other factors. He uses these factors to draw conclusions about why some societies became centralized, complex, and technologically sophisticated while others did not. He looks at archaeological evidence such as the remains of plants and animals to identify which crops were domesticated,* where, and at what times.

His argument always proceeds from physical evidence (characteristics such as natural docility or rapid growth rate) to social conclusions (cultures that could domesticate animals had access to more advantages), and he bases his argument on comparisons.

Contribution in Context

Diamond was not the first man–land* geographer—that is, a geographer whose analysis considers the environmental context of historical events—to look at the broad distinctions that have set human societies on their different paths, nor the first to look for ultimate causes in the deep recesses of prehistory.

In his 1972 book *The Colombian Exchange*, the American historian Alfred Crosby* reflected on the process of intercontinental exchange between the Old World (Asia, Africa, and Europe) and the New (the Americas, Australia). Crosby's account of the meeting of the Old and New Worlds has similarities to Diamond's. "When Columbus* arrived, even the most advanced [Native Americans] were barely out of the Stone Age,* and their armies were swept aside by tiny bands of conquistadors."* Furthermore, they had "few domesticated animals," and "died in droves of diseases" that had become commonplace in the Old World.[6]

The focus of Crosby's argument, however, is only partly on how Europeans came to dominate the world. Much of his book is dedicated to tracking the consequences of the sudden bringing together of two landmasses separated for millennia; many of these consequences were biological: some species became extinct while others spread around the world. In other words, Crosby is interested in the ways in which the powerful Europeans brought their crops and animals across the sea, and brought back others from the Americas.

Diamond is more interested in the original conditions that allowed the Europeans to be in this position. So although his work may share Crosby's focus in many ways, his contribution lies in the scale and scope of the proof of his theory.

NOTES

1   Jared Diamond, *Guns, Germs, and Steel: The Fates of Human Societies* (New York: W. W. Norton & Company, 1999), 25.

2   Diamond, *Guns, Germs, and Steel*, 24.

3   Diamond, *Guns, Germs, and Steel*, 37.

4   Diamond, *Guns, Germs, and Steel*, 408.

5   Diamond, *Guns, Germs, and Steel*, 424.

6   Alfred W. Crosby, *The Colombian Exchange: Biological and Cultural Consequences of 1492* (Westport, CT: Praeger, 2003), 21.

SECTION 2
IDEAS

MODULE 5
MAIN IDEAS

KEY POINTS

- The key themes of *Guns, Germs, and Steel* are the distribution of natural goods and features throughout the world; the role of those resources in encouraging agriculture; and the role of agriculture in encouraging development.

- Eurasia had the right mix of crops, animals, and geographical features to encourage settlement in cities, and therefore complexity (guns and steel) and robust immune systems (germs); the rest of the world did not.

- Diamond wrote this book for a popular, rather than an academic, audience, and it led to some criticism that the book is not rigorous enough.

Key Themes

The key themes of Jared Diamond's *Guns, Germs, and Steel* concern some of the most basic building blocks of civilization. The core argument concerns the naturally unequal distribution of crops such as wheat that are easy to cultivate and animals such as the goat that are easy to domesticate.* This unevenness meant that people living in different regions experienced different developmental paths.

Diamond's overall question is: what are the *ultimate* causes of inequality between regions of the world? The themes he explores are natural—crops, animals, and terrain. In Eurasia, these factors gave rise to both social complexity and disease, and thereby set the stage for these societies, and particularly those of Western Europe, to dominate the rest of the world.

> 66 When Pizarro* and Atahuallpa* met at Cajamarca,*
> why did Pizarro capture Atahuallpa and kill so many
> of his followers, instead of Atahuallpa's vastly more
> numerous forces capturing and killing Pizarro? After all,
> Pizarro had only 62 soldiers mounted on horses, along
> with 106 foot soldiers, while Atahuallpa commanded an
> army of about 80,000. 99
>
> Jared Diamond, *Guns, Germs, and Steel*

Understanding Diamond's aim in *Guns, Germs, and Steel* means understanding, too, the difference between "proximate" causes—an apple falls from a tree because it is shaken by a stiff breeze, for example—and "ultimate" causes—the causes that might explain why *that* apple fell when other apples on nearby trees did not. The "ultimate" cause may be that the tree that shed apples was on a poor patch of land without much nutrition, and the stems attaching the apples to the tree were weaker. Both answers are right. But one is more comprehensive.

Exploring the Ideas

Diamond's overall argument is that today's profoundly unequal world is the result of geographic inequalities in the natural world, rather than genetic inequalities such as some peoples having higher intelligence than others. These geographic inequalities include both crops and animals that lend themselves to domestication (the process by which wild animals and plants are "tamed" by selective breeding for features that serve human beings) and features of the terrain.

Europeans, for instance, became advanced at warfare because their continent is naturally broken up by mountains and rivers into small societies that were prone to conflict. Rather than hunting and gathering naturally occurring food, the fertile land and access to fresh water in Europe allowed for "food production," which "was indirectly a prerequisite for the development of guns, germs, and steel."[1]

Food production was not, Diamond argues, "invented" by some clever people around the world who had a better idea than hunting and gathering—rather it "evolved" slowly.[2] Several factors underlie the origins of food production. The availability of crops that are easily domesticated is one. Oats, for instance, require little in the way of selective breeding to make them easily farmed, whereas corn requires a great deal. Crops were domesticated to yield larger amounts of food. Similarly, dogs were domesticated to be docile and friendly to their masters.

Eurasia started off with many easily domesticated staple crops—wheat, barley, lentils, and so forth—whereas the Americas did not. Moreover, a complete package is necessary to make the switch worthwhile. This means there must be enough high-yielding cereal crops, large land animals to work the fields (and eventually become a food source themselves), and a temperate climate.* "The reason," Diamond argues, "Native Americans did not domesticate apples lay with the entire suite of wild plant and animal species available to Native Americans"; there was only modest potential for domestication available to them.[3] Domesticating plants and animals involves a fundamental change in ways of life—so for any to occur at all, it must be very worthwhile.

How does food production give rise to guns, germs, and steel? Food production supports dense populations, which in turn "led to the proximate causes of germs, literacy, technology, and centralized government." And this led to Eurasian world domination.[4] When humans live close to animals, and close to one another in cities, diseases can readily make the jump across species and quickly become commonplace among entire populations (smallpox, for instance, originated in cattle).[5] Density, however, begets technology as well as germs. "A stored food surplus" in an agricultural society "can support

... full time specialists," from kings and bureaucrats to blacksmiths, scholars, and soldiers.[6] Conversely, in communities that live by hunting and gathering, everyone is required to spend many hours in finding and processing food. So the scribes and blacksmiths of agricultural societies have the time to develop new inventions—writing systems, tools, and weapons—that pave the way for yet more advanced inventions.

Diamond calls this an "autocatalytic" process, which simply means that it is a process that builds on itself: bronze working allows humans to use more advanced tools to mine iron, which allows them to make yet more advanced tools. Therefore, we come to see how food production "makes complex societies possible."[7] Eurasia was naturally, and arbitrarily, endowed with the geographical features that give rise to food production. This in turn gave rise to technology, which enabled more advanced technology and the exchanges of ideas with other complex societies—which gave rise to further advancement.

Language and Expression

Guns, Germs, and Steel was written for a mass audience—most reviewers praised "its erudition, clear prose, and elegant synthesis of multiple sources, from archaeology to zoology."[8] Diamond uses colorful examples generously, explains academic concepts throughout, and does not use overlong or complicated sentences. Moreover, he uses graphs throughout the book to illustrate complex concepts—especially worthwhile is the graphical summary of his entire model of ultimate causes of history, compressed into a single page.[9]

Although the book is highly readable and engaging, it has been criticized for its lack of academic referencing. While Diamond presents a "further reading list" at the end of the work, there are few, if any, citations in the text. Some reviewers have criticized *Guns, Germs, and Steel* for getting its facts wrong, and focusing on making an elegant argument that would appeal to a mass audience (and the judges of literary prizes), rather than an academically rigorous one.[10]

Students reading *Guns, Germs, and Steel* should keep in mind that Diamond is balancing commercial appeal and academic rigor.

NOTES

1   Jared Diamond, *Guns, Germs, and Steel: The Fates of Human Societies* (New York: W. W. Norton & Company, 1999), 86.

2   Diamond, *Guns, Germs, and Steel*, 104.

3   Diamond, *Guns, Germs, and Steel*, 156.

4   Diamond, *Guns, Germs, and Steel*, 195.

5   Diamond, *Guns, Germs, and Steel*, 207.

6   Diamond, *Guns, Germs, and Steel*, 90.

7   Diamond, *Guns, Germs, and Steel*, 286.

8   Robin McKie, "Jared Diamond: What We Can Learn from Tribal Life," *Guardian*, January 6, 2013, accessed July 17, 2015, http://www. theguardian.com/science/2013/jan/06/jared-diamond-tribal-life-anthropology.

9   Diamond, *Guns, Germs, and Steel*, 87.

10 Andrew Sluyter, "Neo-Environmental Determinism, Intellectual Damage Control, and Nature/Society Science," *Antipode* 35, no. 4 (2003): 813.

MODULE 6
SECONDARY IDEAS

KEY POINTS

- Eurasia was destined to dominate because of its basket of natural goods; Europe was destined to dominate within this system because of its terrain features.

- China is too geographically and politically unified to develop dependably; bad decisions made by emperors tend not to get reversed.

- Although Diamond's book is remembered more for its content than its methodology, recent scholarship has become interested in exploring natural experiments.*

Other Ideas

Jared Diamond's key themes in *Guns, Germs, and Steel* concern the global history of development based on environmental factors. His secondary ideas relate to how particular areas of the Old World developed differently—he focuses in particular on China and Africa. The Old World, after all, was geographically linked—and food production arose indigenously in Africa and China.

There is another key factor here, however: the advantages of an East–West orientation. "As one moves along a north–south axis," he writes, "one traverses zones differing greatly" in terms of climate, native species of plants and animals, and terrain. This made it hard to share both domesticated* plants and animals and technology; along an East–West axis where the climate remains broadly consistent, however, it is much simpler.[1]

This observation leads Diamond to another interesting question. Both Europe and China sat along the East–West axis of Eurasia, and

> ❝ A larger area or population means more potential
> inventors, more competing societies, more innovations
> available to adopt—and more pressure to adopt and
> retain innovations, because societies failing to do so will
> tend to be eliminated by competing societies. ❞
>
> Jared Diamond, *Guns, Germs, and Steel*

both enjoyed indigenous food production and rapid technological advance. So what explains historical European dominance? To answer the question, Diamond turns to the way that geography affects politics in complex societies.

Exploring the Ideas

"Until around A.D. 1450," Diamond argues, "China was technologically much more innovative and advanced than Europe [but] then ceased to be innovative."[2] Diamond lays out a number of proximate causes rooted in European society: the development of a merchant class and the economic system of capitalism;* patent protection for inventions; its comparative lack of political regimes founded on absolute despotism* (that is, where power was concentrated in very few hands) and crushing taxation; and its Greco-Judeo-Christian tradition of empirical* inquiry"[3] (that is, the scientific tradition of basing conclusions on observable evidence).

Again, the ultimate causes behind these proximate causes, Diamond finds, are geographical—and political unity is key to this problem. China, as a society, was too unified. This meant that temporary "backward" or poor decisions become permanent; Diamond cites a political dispute in the Chinese court leading to the permanent dismantling of its ocean-going fleet in the fifteenth century.[4] Europe, on the other hand, was politically fragmented—so, if one society made a backward decision, it was likely another would learn from it. Diamond gives the example of the Italian explorer Christopher Columbus,* who "succeeded on his fifth try in persuading one of Europe's hundreds of princes to sponsor" his voyage across the Atlantic.[5]

In other words, China's structure meant mistakes made by rulers would be implemented across the entire country, whereas Europe's structure meant that while several princes might not see the value of the voyage, eventually one would. Then, as others became aware of the success of the first voyage, "best practice" would ensure they would naturally want to follow in those footsteps.

What is the geographic basis of Europe's fragmentation? It is a continent divided by rivers, peninsulas, islands, and mountains, and so "Europe has many scattered small core areas, none big enough to dominate the others for long, and each the center of chronically independent states."[6] China, on the other hand, has only two—comparatively small—islands, and was unified by 221 B.C.E. Its divided nature meant Europe only began the process of unification in the twentieth century—and even now, it is a far from assured process.[7] Diamond argues that China's connectedness was an advantage at first, as it could devote vast resources to developing a complex, advanced society. However, Europe's structure meant that "if one state did not pursue some particular innovation, another did, forcing neighboring states to do likewise" or face domination, economically or militarily.[8]

Overlooked

Guns, Germs, and Steel is a notably cohesive work in terms of its argument and structure. In the light of this, it is its methodology of "history-as-science" rather than its content that has been somewhat overlooked.

The American psychologist Stuart Vyse* thinks Diamond's scientific approach to understanding social outcomes has benefits for other disciplines. Behavior analysis, he says, "could be introduced into new areas of public dialogue if more behavior analysts followed Diamond's lead and conducted scientific histories."[9] Vyse suggests that social problems with behavioral rather than genetic origins "such as aggression, crime, and alcohol and drug addiction" may be affected by important environmental factors that are "yet to be articulated."[10] Diamond's method using grand comparisons is, for Vyse, a way to obtain real knowledge about social realities without the need for laboratory conditions.* While the tradition of "natural experiments" in social analysis has a long history, and is well rooted in policy analysis today, Diamond has done much, Vyse says, to prove that it can be applied on yet grander scales.

One example of such an application was a natural experiment by David Humphreys* and colleagues at the University of Oxford. They used existing data to evaluate a new rule about the sale of alcohol in the British city of Manchester to investigate whether the removal of regulations on the time of day alcohol is sold would lead to an increase in anti-social behavior. Police incident reports before and after the rule change provided a means to measure the change. Their conclusion was that an increase in incidents late at night occurred after the rule change (but not an increase overall). This is not a controlled experiment, but a "natural" experiment, making use of the wider world to draw conclusions about the proximate and ultimate causes of social outcomes.[11]

NOTES

1   Jared Diamond, *Guns, Germs, and Steel: The Fates of Human Societies* (New York: W. W. Norton & Company, 1999), 399.

2   Diamond, *Guns, Germs, and Steel*, 253.

3   Diamond, *Guns, Germs, and Steel*, 410.

4   Diamond, *Guns, Germs, and Steel*, 412.

5   Diamond, *Guns, Germs, and Steel*, 413.

6   Diamond, *Guns, Germs, and Steel*, 414.

7   Diamond, *Guns, Germs, and Steel*, 414.

8   Diamond, *Guns, Germs, and Steel*, 416.

9   Stuart Vyse, "World History for Behavior Analysts: Jared Diamond's *Guns, Germs, and Steel*," *Behavior and Social Issues* 11, no. 1 (2001): 85.

10   Vyse, "World History for Behavior Analysts," 86.

11   David K. Humphreys et al., "Evaluating the Impact of Flexible Alcohol Trading Hours on Violence: An Interrupted Time Series Analysis," *PLOS ONE* 8, no. 2 (2013): 1, accessed July 15, 2015, doi:10.1371/journal.pone.0055581.

MODULE 7
ACHIEVEMENT

KEY POINTS

- Diamond's theory in *Guns, Germs, and Steel* is one of the most rigorous theories of world history.
- Some critics argue that this is not a real theory, but a backward-looking justification of existing distributions of power.
- Critics argue that some groups Diamond claims were eradicated by Europeans actually still exist.

Assessing the Argument

Is the "grand" theory of Jared Diamond's *Guns, Germs, and Steel* convincing? The answer is both "yes" and "no." It is possible that Diamond does not actually derive any laws at all—he merely explains what has already happened. So, the Old World conquers the New, and Europe emerges victorious as though it could only have happened this way. This question—whether or not history, as a discipline, lends itself to parsimonious* explanations—is asked by the right-wing economist Gene Callahan* of the Ludwig von Mises Institute,*[1] an organization that argues for less government interference in the free market.

"Parsimony" in this context means that a complex set of outcomes can be explained with reference to one critically important factor—in this case, Diamond explains all of human history with reference to the distribution of a very few factors. Callahan suggests that parsimonious explanations are possible in the natural sciences—an apple, released from a height, will always fall—"but no similar facts are given to the historian."[2]

Whether or not laws actually govern history and other social

> 66 While Diamond's book is filled with valuable insights, it is not, as he would like to believe, the first step in the reformation of history along more 'scientific' lines, but only another interesting vantage point from which to contemplate humanity's past. Furthermore, the policy implications of his overreach are a danger to both human welfare and freedom. 99
>
> Gene Callahan, "The Diamond Fallacy"

sciences is still up for debate. Assuming that it *is* possible for history to be governed by laws, then Diamond's argument is successful. This would also assume that because things happened in a certain way, they could not have happened any other way over the long term. But if by "history" we mean a succession of singular events affecting one another in unpredictable ways, then the grand theory of *Guns, Germs, and Steel* is not successful.

Achievement in Context

Diamond's *Guns, Germs, and Steel* was an enormously successful book. It won the prestigious Pulitzer Prize* for General Nonfiction in 1998, and has been translated into 36 languages. In the United States, the National Geographic Society produced a TV series based on the book which was broadcast in 2005. What is more telling, though, is that it won the Phi Beta Kappa Award in Science in 1997— an award given to works of science literature, which lends support to Diamond's claim that history (and geography) can genuinely be a science.

In their review of the book, "Diamond in the Rough," the American sociologists Richard York* and Philip Mancus* speculate why it was that *Guns, Germs, and Steel* had such commercial success but relatively little direct impact on the discipline of environmental sociology,* especially given its high level of scientific rigor. "This is ironic," they say, "since environmental sociology ... is fundamentally concerned with how human societies are both affected by and affect their environments."[3]

Diamond's parsimonious scientific perspective was one reason for this lack of impact. It was in stark contrast to another phenomenon in the social sciences often called the "cultural turn," which came into prominence in the early 1990s. The cultural turn—described as "one of the most influential trends in the humanities and social sciences in the last generation" by the American sociologists Mark Jacobs* and Lyn Spillman*—sees social science as a tool for exploring meanings in specific contexts, rather than deriving universal laws.[4] In effect, Diamond's ideas were out of step with current trends. As a result, Diamond's work went on to be more influential in development economics than sociology.

Limitations

The American anthropologist Michael Wilcox* argues that many people would find *Guns, Germs, and Steel* (and *Collapse*, a later book) ridiculous. His reasoning is that Diamond ignores the perspectives of people he claims were completely eradicated, such as Native Americans, even though they continue to exist today, albeit in a different way. He argues that the idea that Native American societies have "collapsed" is actually a popular myth—"the popular narratives of conquest and disappearance are just that—a mythology."[5] He asks, "What if archaeologists were asked to explain the continued presence of descendant communities five hundred years after Columbus,* instead of their disappearance or marginality?"[6]

Wilcox argues that Diamond's "terminal narratives"—the idea that native communities reached an "end" when colonization* occurred—are not just questionable in their accuracy, but incredibly damaging to the psyche of the remaining native communities. In the "terminal" narrative, "abandoned sites" of native cities are interpreted as evidence of social collapse. Wilcox counters that "[the] other interpretation is one that envisions archaeological sites the way Native peoples see them: as part of a living cosmological and historical landscape," still inhabited by native peoples.[7]

The core of Wilcox's discussion of the limitations of *Guns, Germs, and Steel* is perspective: Diamond assumes that native culture collapsed, and is now an artifact of the past, but this denies the existence of still-living Native Americans. Clearly, Native Americans would reject his thesis.

NOTES

1   Gene Callahan, "The Diamond Fallacy," Mises Institute, accessed May 17, 2015, https://mises.org/library/diamond-fallacy.

2   Callahan, "The Diamond Fallacy."

3   Richard York and Philip Mancus, "Diamond in the Rough: Reflections on *Guns, Germs, and Steel*," *Research in Human Ecology* 14, no. 2 (2007): 157.

4   Mark D. Jacobs and Lyn Spillman, "Cultural Sociology at the Crossroads of a Discipline," *Poetics* 33 (2005): 1

5   Michael Wilcox, "Marketing Conquest and the Vanishing Indian: An Indigenous Response to Jared Diamond's *Guns, Germs, and Steel*," *Journal of Social Archaeology* 10, no. 1 (2010): 96.

6   Michael Wilcox, *The Pueblo Revolt and the Mythology of Conquest: An Indigenous Archaeology* (Berkeley: University of California Press, 2009), 11.

7   Wilcox, *The Pueblo Revolt*, 96.

MODULE 8
PLACE IN THE AUTHOR'S WORK

KEY POINTS

- Jared Diamond's three most famous books—*The Third Chimpanzee, Guns, Germs, and Steel, and Collapse*—are all about identifying the most important factors that drive change.

- All of Diamond's work is notable for its rigorous use of the "natural experiments"* of the comparative method.

- *Guns, Germs, and Steel* is Diamond's most famous book, and has been lauded with awards and translated into 36 languages.

Positioning

Although he is now much better known for his non-technical work, Jared Diamond was not always an author of popular books for a mass audience; his publications before *Guns, Germs, and Steel* were academic articles in specialist journals.

Diamond's first popular book—*The Third Chimpanzee*—was published in 1991. Like *Guns, Germs, and Steel*, it was a book intended for a general audience. Also, much like *Guns, Germs, and Steel*, it was concerned with how humanity came to dominate the world. In *The Third Chimpanzee*, Diamond focuses on the roots of human behavior in our evolutionary history. For example, he notes a "great leap forward" that occurred in the last 60,000 years involving the abrupt development of trade, culture, and (comparative) technological sophistication. This took place among anatomically modern humans, and Diamond suggests it was a result of the development of our ability to talk.[1] Language allowed humans to "brainstorm together about

> 66 Of course it's not true that all societies are doomed
> to collapse because of environmental damage: in the
> past some societies did while others didn't; the real
> question is why only some societies proved fragile, and
> what distinguished those that collapsed from those
> that didn't. 99
>
> Jared Diamond, *Collapse*

how to devise a better tool, or about what a cave painting might mean."[2]

Diamond's most significant work after *Guns, Germs, and Steel* was *Collapse: How Societies Choose to Fail or Survive* in 2005. While *The Third Chimpanzee* focused on evolution and *Guns, Germs, and Steel* focused on environments in which societies emerge, *Collapse* focused on what happens once societies are formed. By, "collapse," Diamond means "a drastic decrease in human population size and/or political, social, economic, or social complexity, over a considerable area, for an extended time."[3]

Integration

What is distinctive about all of Diamond's work—especially the trilogy of *The Third Chimpanzee*, *Guns, Germs, and Steel*, and *Collapse*— is the scientific approach they share. For Diamond science is not defined as experiments in laboratory conditions,* but rather, "the acquisition of reliable knowledge about the world" in whatever way possible.[4] Moreover, in all his work, Diamond points his science in the same direction: the acquisition of reliable knowledge of the *long-term* factors, biological, environmental, and cultural, that have determined what the world looks like today, and what it may look like in future.

One of the key differences between Diamond's early work and

Collapse is the importance of structure (the pattern of circumstances and institutions) and agency (independent choice) in shaping behavior. *Collapse* has a central role for human choice. Some societies, writes Diamond, succeeded in "solving extremely difficult environmental problems" by learning from experience and adapting their behavior to interact with their environments properly. This might be by controlling their populations, by finding new sources of food, or careful land management.[5] This is why Diamond includes the all-important word "choose" in the title of the book.

Collapse and *Guns, Germs, and Steel*, in particular, can be read as emphasizing two distinct factors (structure and agency) that have defined the development of human societies since prehistory. *Guns, Germs, and Steel* focuses on "buildups," whereas *Collapse* looks at the other end—shut down. Seeing Diamond's work as unified helps illustrate the explanatory power of taking a macro view—meaning focusing on the large scale and the long term—on societies to understand universal principles.

Significance

In all his writing, Diamond has demonstrated his ability to weave together information from a diverse spectrum of disciplines and explain it to a broad readership. He has won a popular following, including such public figures as the entrepreneur and philanthropist Bill Gates,* and has a role in ongoing debates over global development. With *Guns, Germs, and Steel* and its follow-up works, Diamond has increased his global reputation as an important voice with a unique integrated perspective of human history and ecology.

Much new information has become available since *Guns, Germs, and Steel* was first published, which Diamond claims has "enriched our understanding without fundamentally changing interpretations."[6] He stands by his main argument that continental environmental differences shaped the patterns of human history and he believes that the themes discussed in the text are still relevant to conversations about global development today.

Guns, Germs, and Steel made Jared Diamond a household name and continues to be the most widely recognized of his works. It has been adopted as a modern classic with a place in the coursework of many colleges and high schools around the world.

NOTES

1 Jared Diamond, *The Rise and Fall of the Third Chimpanzee* (London: Vintage, 2002), 46.

2 Diamond, *The Rise and Fall of the Third Chimpanzee*, 47.

3 Jared Diamond, *Collapse: How Societies Choose to Fail or Survive* (London: Penguin, 2005), 3.

4 Diamond, *Collapse*, 17.

5 Diamond, *Collapse*, 10.

6 Jared Diamond, "Guns, Germs, and Steel: The Fates of Human Societies," accessed September 6, 2013, http://www.jareddiamond.org/Jared_Diamond/Guns,_Germs,_and_Steel.html.

SECTION 3
IMPACT

MODULE 9
THE FIRST RESPONSES

KEY POINTS

- Critics have argued that Diamond was wrong because his theory and its general assumptions "excuse" the crimes of European colonialism.*
- Diamond responds by suggesting that a scientific approach to history requires generalization.
- Diamond and his critics represent two opposing views of academia, what it should do and be, and the relative importance of scientific rigor.

Criticism

Jared Diamond's *Guns, Germs, and* Steel has been widely criticized for making many Eurocentric* assumptions (that is, it founds its arguments on ideas of European preeminence).

The American anthropologist James Blaut* argued that the book "is influential in part because its Eurocentric arguments seem, to a general reader, to be so compellingly 'scientific.'"[1] Blaut argues, largely, that Diamond has taken the way the world is today as inevitable—there was no other way history could go—and so he is attempting to justify it after the fact. Blaut's fundamental critique is of Diamond's explanation of the reasons Europe, rather than Eurasia generally, became globally dominant. He points out that the spread of technology is a key aspect of Eurasia's rise, until it comes to Europe's predominance.

The argument that "Europe had just the right balance between too little differentiation and too much" presents a problem because it means Diamond, based purely on a backward-looking justification of European dominance, is able to set his own boundary between "too

> 66 I dispute Diamond's argument not because he tries to use scientific data and scientific reasoning to solve the problems of human history. That is laudable. But he claims to produce reliable, scientific answers to these problems when in fact he does not have such answers, and he resolutely ignores the findings of social science while advancing old and discredited theories of environmental determinism. That is bad science. 99
>
> James Blaut, "Environmentalism and Eurocentrism"

little" and "too much."[2] In essence, Blaut's criticism of *Guns, Germs, and Steel* is that it was not a genuine attempt at a theory that could predict outcomes, but, rather, it made the existing distribution of power in the world look "natural."

The anthropologists Frederick Errington* and Deborah Gewertz* respond directly to Diamond in their 2004 book *Yali's Question*, named after the question posed by the New Guinean politician Yali* to Jared Diamond: "Why is it that you white people developed so much cargo and brought it to New Guinea, but we black people had little cargo of our own?"[3] "We find it problematic," they write, "that history's grand course can be adequately understood without considering culturally grounded ideas about what life is and might become."[4] Errington and Gewertz believe, in other words, that Diamond misunderstood Yali's question. Yali was not interested in the really great things that Western people invented. He was concerned about "Western condescension that allowed Europeans to deny Papua New Guineans fundamental worth."[5] In other words, Yali is questioning why Westerners hold all the power while New Guineans (and others in the developing world) are chronically disadvantaged. Diamond's answer, from this point of view, seems more like an excuse than an explanation—Westerners could not help conquering the world, and the resulting distribution of power is an inevitable consequence of geography.[6]

Ultimately, Errington and Gewertz's objection is about agency: just because one society *does* develop guns and steel, we should not conclude that they always conquer. The assumption that they will presupposes that all humans are self-regarding and acquisitive—but this is not a universal account of human nature. "Europeans had the resources and inclination to treat Yali and other Papua New Guineas with contempt," they write, but just because they could, does not mean they should be absolved.[7] In other words, individual choice must be brought back into the picture.

Responses

Diamond's response to his critics was that they had misinterpreted his position—"our differences arise from the different historical scales that we consider."[8] In essence, Diamond's critics suggested that he did not leave enough space for culture and self-determination in his theory. His response to this was that the boundaries of what can be determined by culture are set by long-term history. Writing of the period following the last Ice Age,* which ended some 12,000 years ago, he writes, "Over the hundreds of generations of post-Ice Age human history, and over a large continent's thousands of societies, cultural differences become sifted to approach limits imposed by environmental constraints."[9] Diamond is writing history from the most general perspective possible. Consequently, he needs to make some assumptions that underplay the role of individuals—but what he gains is the ability to describe universal trends.

Diamond suggests that the approach of his critics is effective for asking specific questions about specific events at specific times. One cannot say for sure why World War II* occurred when, where, and how it did without exploring the particulars of Germany's relationship with the rest of Europe and the Treaty of Versailles.* However; to ask questions of the widest generality—"Why was Europe so industrially advanced at the time of World War II compared to the rest of the world?" for example—one needs a theory that works on the widest of scales.

Conflict and Consensus

The debate between Diamond and his critics did not result in any positions shifting; they disagreed fundamentally about what academia is supposed to do and be. In essence, Diamond sees his academic mission as presenting a dispassionate, purely factual account of human history for 13,000 years. This means he denies agent-driven accounts (where societies are seen as the expression of different groups of people's independent choices), which do not necessarily purport to "rank" societies in order of their successful adaptation to structure. His critics, such as Errington and Gewertz, suggest he does not value societies that fail to become world-dominant, even though those societies may be the expression of the cultural preferences of those who live in them (e.g., that hunter-gatherer* tribes may value their lifestyles, and not see themselves as simply unlucky or failed).

This debate continues with Diamond's most recent work, *The World Until Yesterday*. In this book, he writes that "traditional societies represent thousands of millennia-long natural experiments in organizing human lives."[10] Canadian anthropologist Wade Davis's* review of the book criticized Diamond's inability to accept humanity's diversity; "the other peoples of the world are not failed attempts at modernity, let alone failed attempts to be us," he writes.[11] In other words, a tribe that either dies out or gets subsumed into another tribe represents two very different things for theorists like Diamond and Davis. For Diamond, they represent alternatives that did not work; for Davis, they represent the unique expression of those people's identity at that place and time. These points of view are both right. But they stem from fundamentally different—and mutually exclusive— perspectives.

NOTES

1 James Blaut, "Environmentalism and Eurocentrism," *Geographical Review* 89, no. 3 (1999): 403.

2 Blaut, "Environmentalism and Eurocentrism," 403.

3 Jared Diamond, *Guns, Germs, and Steel: The Fates of Human Societies* (New York: W. W. Norton & Company, 1999), 14.

4 Frederick Errington and Deborah Gewrtz, *Yali's Question: Sugar, Culture, and History* (Chicago: University of Chicago Press, 2004), 7.

5 Errington and Gewrtz, *Yali's Question*, 8.

6 Errington and Gewrtz, *Yali's Question*, 9.

7 Errington and Gewertz. *Yali's Question*, 14.

8 Jared Diamond, "Guns, Germs, and Steel," *New York Review of Books*, June 26, 1997, accessed May 23, 2015, http://www.nybooks.com/articles/archives/1997/jun/26/guns-germs-and-steel/.

9 Diamond, "Guns, Germs, and Steel."

10 Jared Diamond, *The World Until Yesterday: What Can We Learn from Traditional Societies?* (London: Penguin, 2013), 32.

11 Wade Davis, "The World Until Yesterday by Jared Diamond: A Review," *Guardian*, January 9, 2013, accessed May 23, 2015, http://www.theguardian.com/books/2013/jan/09/history-society.

MODULE 10
THE EVOLVING DEBATE

KEY POINTS

- *Guns, Germs, and Steel* has become part of a scientific approach to economic development based on the search for laws and principles.
- The field of development economics compares a country's natural resources endowments with its chances of economic success.
- The writing of the American economist Jeffrey Sachs* is perhaps the most influential in this school of literature, especially Sachs's concept of the "resource curse."

Uses and Problems

Debates in geography, politics, and economics (especially economic development) turn on some of the points Diamond raises in *Guns, Germs, and Steel*, even if only implicitly. On the one hand, there is the mainstream "empiricist" or "positivist" approach; aiming to be scientific, with the use of statistics and technical information, it is an approach that makes generalizations and is associated with institutions like the World Bank.*[1] On the other hand, approaches that focus more on the role of ideas and culture sit outside the mainstream. They suggest that more "scientific" theories implicitly justify the domination of the developed world over the developing one and are "unwittingly invested in a set of persistent discourses that point to the need for change *over there*, rather than *over here*."[2]

There are key parallels between Diamond's 2005 book *Collapse* and the important United Nations* publication *A Guide to the World's Resources 2005*, for example. "It has long been suspected," Diamond

> 66 The livelihoods of the poor can be enhanced by capturing greater value from ecosystems. But this can only happen where good governance practices prevail. That means managing ecosystems sustainably and ensuring the poor access, voice, and participation. In other words, there is power in nature for poverty reduction, but only if we deal effectively with the nature of power—the governance over resources—so that the poor can reap the benefits of ecosystems. 99
>
> Gregory Mock, *A Guide to the World's Resources*

writes, "[that societies collapse because] people inadvertently [destroyed] the environmental resources on which their societies depended."[3] He suggests that the environmental problems that lead societies to collapse are "deforestation and habitat destruction, soil problems ... water management problems ... overhunting, overfishing, effects of introduced species on native species, human population growth, and increased per capita* impact of people."[4]

Effectively, this is a list of the mistakes people make in their relationships with their environment. The *Resources* report opens by declaring that "[the] ecosystems of the world represent the natural capital stock of the planet," and "over the last 50 years, we have changed ecosystems more rapidly than at any time in human history, largely to meet growing demands for food, freshwater, timber, and fiber."[5] They suggest "this requires that the poor manage ecosystems so that they support stable productivity over time."[6] This idea—that environment, politics, and economic development are all connected, and that there is "one correct answer" to diagnose and solve the problem—is at one with Diamond's analysis, and continues to be important.

Schools of Thought

Diamond's work played an important role in helping define some of the problems historically tackled by economists who address developing economies.

In an article published in 1971, the development economist Paul Streeten* outlined the problem. The most striking fact of underdevelopment* today is that underdeveloped states "lie in the tropical* and semi-tropical zones," and that considering this a coincidence adds to the problem. He cites "a deep-seated optimistic bias with which we approach problems of development and the reluctance to admit the vast differences in initial conditions" faced by underdeveloped states.[7]

The American economist David Landes,* meanwhile, outlines a number of environmental conditions that lead to uneven development;* he focuses on the role of heat in encouraging more infectious disease and making work more difficult.[8]

One of the most important works in economic development to embrace Diamond's perspective of the relationship between geography and economic outcomes is by the economists John Gallup,* Jeffrey Sachs, and Andrew Mellinger.* In their survey of all the world's countries on the basis of their geographical situation and political history (for example, were they led by a dictator?), they looked at average income by nation. They found that "there are 23 countries with the most favored combination of geography and politics— Northern hemisphere, temperate* zone, coastal, non-socialist, non-war torn—with an average [income] of $18,000."[9] Being located in the tropics, not being located on a coast, being in the Southern hemisphere, and other similar criteria, were shown to reduce the predicted average income of a country by tens of thousands of dollars per capita.[10]

In Current Scholarship

Perhaps the most prominent thinker today who shares Diamond's point of view about the importance of the environment on human outcomes is the economist Jeffrey Sachs. In his article "Institutions Matter, but Not for Everything," Sachs argues that human factors (broadly defined as "institutions" and including everything from traditions to governments) account for only a part of economic development. Sachs distances himself from environmental determinism* (that is, the view that environmental factors decide everything as far as development is concerned), arguing that even if good health were "important to development," then an area climatically prone to malaria* will have special difficulties—but it will not be condemned to poverty forever.[11] Sachs concludes that environmental factors define the particular challenges states face in development. To imagine that all problems are either caused by "bad institutions" or by the exploitation of poor countries by rich countries ignores these important factors.[12]

One of the most important environmental factors Sachs identified (alongside the American economist Andrew Warner*) was the so-called "resource curse"—a phenomenon whereby countries with abundant natural resources, which should allow them to prosper economically, actually fail to develop or end up with very poor governance and social problems. There is currently no clear agreement on *how* the natural resource curse stops development, but one of Sachs and Warner's arguments is that, while the extraction and sale of abundant natural resources may generate income, it does not build a country's wider economy.[13] In other words, a country with oil can sell it in partnership with foreign oil companies and does not develop its own native industries. When the oil runs out, there are few native industries—such as those that export valuable, manufactured goods—to take over.

Unlike Diamond, Sachs is not interested in the consequences of 13,000 years of history, but the two share a key interest in how environmental conditions shape and constrain the choices societies make.

NOTES

1   Maureen Hickey and Vicky Lawson, "Beyond Science? Human Geography, Interpretation, and Critique," in *Questioning Geography: Fundamental Debates*, ed. Noel Castree et al. (Malden, MA: Blackwell, 2005), 110.

2   Hickey and Lawson, "Beyond Science?" 109.

3   Jared Diamond, *Collapse: How Societies Choose to Fail or Survive* (London: Penguin, 2005), 4.

4   Diamond, *Collapse*, 4.

5   Gregory Mock, ed., *A Guide to World Resources 2005* (Washington, DC: World Resources Institute, 2005), 4.

6   Mock, *A Guide to World Resources*, 7.

7   Paul Streeten, "How Poor Are the Poor Countries?" in *Development in a Divided World*, ed. D. Seers and L. Joy (Harmondsworth: Penguin, 1971), 78.

8   David Landes, *The Wealth and Poverty of Nations: Why Some Are So Rich and Some Are So Poor* (New York: W. W. Norton & Company, 1998), 7–11.

9   John Gallup et al., *Geography and Economic Development* (Cambridge: National Bureau of Economic Research, 1998), 8.

10 Gallup et al., *Geography and Economic Development*, 8.

11 Jeffrey Sachs, "Institutions Matter, but Not for Everything," *Finance and Development* 40, no. 2 (June 2003): 40.

12 Sachs, "Institutions Matter, but Not for Everything," 38–9.

13 Jeffrey Sachs and Andrew Warner, "The Curse of Natural Resources," *European Economic Review* 45, nos. 4–6 (2001): 833.

MODULE 11
IMPACT AND INFLUENCE TODAY

KEY POINTS

- *Guns, Germs, and Steel* is less directly relevant today than other works that share its scientific methodology (especially in economic development).
- The Canadian economist Nathan Nunn,* for example, argues that there is a strong correlation between the number of slaves taken from certain parts of Africa and current levels of underdevelopment.*
- Critics of this method suggest it is oversimplistic and ignores complex factors such as relationships of dominance, which can determine outcomes more than any "underlying" factor.

Position

Jared Diamond's *Guns, Germs, and Steel* occupies a prominent place on undergraduate reading lists in international history, politics, economics, geography, sociology, and numerous other disciplines. This is, in part, because it is so well written, popular, and accessible.

From an academic standpoint, however, the book is on shakier ground. For example, the American historian Stephen Wertheim,* in a review of *The World Until Yesterday*, wrote, "*Guns, Germs, and Steel* attacked the notion that racial superiority explained Western global pre-eminence, a view taken seriously by almost no one who's taken seriously."[1] The economists Daron Acemoglu* and James Robinson's* influential *Why Nations Fail* takes a more charitable approach: *Guns, Germs, and Steel* "cannot be extended to explain modern world inequality" because it simplifies too much, meaning it cannot address

> 66 Why are the institutions of the United States so much more conducive to economic success than those of Mexico, or for that matter, the rest of Latin America? The answer to this question lies in the way different societies formed during the early colonial* period. An institutional divergence took place then, with implications lasting into the present day. To understand this divergence we must begin right at the foundation of the colonies in North and Latin America. 99
>
> Daron Acemoglu and James Robinson, *Why Nations Fail*

why "the average Spaniard is more than six times richer than the average Peruvian," and how to rectify the situation.[2]

Guns, Germs, and Steel is now more relevant for its use of "comparative methodology"* on the grandest of scales (an approach that aims to figure out the effects of given factors on given outcomes by examining two or more cases, their similarities and differences). In *Natural Experiments of History*, a volume Diamond co-edited with the British political theorist James Robinson,* Diamond expanded on this idea and explored its possible uses. "Historical comparisons," the book concludes, "may yield insights that cannot be extracted from a single case study alone" and "when one proposes a conclusion, one may be able to strengthen that conclusion [by using empirical evidence]."[3]

So, why does *Guns, Germs, and Steel* still matter? In part, because it is an accessible and intellectually graspable introduction to the comparative method for undergraduates. As we have seen, perhaps it is for its methodology, more than its conclusions, that it remains so widely read among academics.

Interaction

The challenge Diamond and his fellow scientists of history pose today tends to focus on the difference between cultural anthropology and science.

The economist Nathan Nunn, for example, contributed the chapter "Shackled to the Past: The Causes and Consequences of Africa's Slave Trades" to Diamond and Robinson's *Natural Experiments of History*. In it, Nunn found that the "parts of the continent from which the largest number of slaves were taken in the past are the parts of the continent that are the poorest today."[4] What is most striking about Nunn's findings is the extent of their scientific rigor; Nunn uses "statistical analysis to examine the relationship between the severity of the slave trades and subsequent economic performance for different parts of Africa."[5] His analysis of the slave trade in Africa is large scale—he makes generalizations that mean the experience of, for example, areas that comprise modern Zimbabwe and the Congo are compared as though they are similar.

Finding a balance between generality and specificity is a serious challenge. Anyone would admit that different areas would have had different experiences of the slave trade. But natural experiments like Nunn's can show that a few common factors—the intensity of the slave trade, for example—have significant power to explain the current conditions of many different peoples.

The Continuing Debate

In the book *Questioning Collapse*, the American anthropologists Patricia McAnany* and Norman Yoffee* bring together a number of responses to Diamond.

The American anthropologists Frederick Errington* and Deborah Gewertz,* meanwhile, updating their arguments from their book *Yali's Question*, which criticizes Diamond's *Guns, Germs, and Steel*, contribute the essay "Excusing the Haves and Blaming the Have Nots in the Telling of History." In it, they argue that "basing history on what appear to be commonsense (Western) suppositions, makes complex political processes into simple, inevitable laws." And basing history on "laws" then makes the current state of affairs look natural.[6]

The problem, they claim, is that this view of history means we do not consider the brutality of the conquistadors* as morally wrong. Factors beyond their control (Eurasian geography and the distribution of plant and animal life) meant the Spanish could not have helped themselves, and the Andean people were doomed from the outset. This is a rejection of the themes that unite *Collapse* and *Guns, Germs, and Steel*. Their argument is that in *Collapse*, Diamond assumes every society "will have an equal capacity to choose"—from cultural factors, to abuse from outside powers, to simply bad luck. For them, this assumption ultimately "clouds our understanding of the processes actually affecting the world today."[7]

Errington and Gewertz give the example of the sugar industries in the United States and Papua New Guinea. The United States subsidizes* its own sugar production (that is, it spends public money to make sure that their sugar is cheap on the open market). "Papua New Guinea's government," on the other hand, "is heavily pressured by the World Bank* and the World Trade Organization"* to be uncompetitive on the open market.[8] This means they cannot subsidize their own sugar industry, nor are they allowed to impose import taxes (called "tariffs") on American sugar. It is not clear how this state of affairs is a result of Papua New Guinea's choices, nor is it clear how the power of the United States in international trade is excusable because it arises from a historical inevitability.

NOTES

1   Stephen Wertheim, "Hunter-Blatherer," *The Nation*, April 22, 2013, 37.

2   Daron Acemoglu and James Robinson, *Why Nations Fail: The Origins of Power, Prosperity, and Poverty* (London: Profile Books, 2012), 52.

3   Jared Diamond and James Robinson, "Afterword," in *Natural Experiments of History*, ed. Jared Diamond and James Robinson (Cambridge, MA: Harvard University Press, 2010), 274.

4   Nathan Nunn, "Shackled to the Past: The Causes and Consequences of Africa's Slave Trades," in *Natural Experiments of History*, ed. Jared Diamond and James Robinson (Cambridge, MA: Harvard University Press, 2010), 142.

5   Nunn, "Shackled to the Past," 146.

6   Frederick Errington and Deborah Gewertz, "Excusing the Haves and Blaming the Have Nots in the Telling of History," in *Questioning Collapse: Human Resilience, Ecological Vulnerability, and the Aftermath of Empire*, ed. Patricia McAnany and Norman Yoffee (Cambridge: Cambridge University Press, 2009), 329–51, 330.

7   Errington and Gewertz, "Excusing the Haves," 341.

8   Errington and Gewertz, "Excusing the Haves," 348–9.

MODULE 12
WHERE NEXT?

KEY POINTS

- *Guns, Germs, and Steel* cemented Diamond's reputation as a public intellectual and he has applied his approach to contemporary problems.
- As Diamond focuses more on culture and methodology, the Anglo-American historian Ian Morris* has taken up the task of explaining *longue durée** history.
- *Guns, Germs, and Steel* provided a scientifically rigorous explanation for the difficult problem of international inequality.

Potential

Jared Diamond's *Guns, Germs, and Steel* is unlikely to continue being influential in itself—the arguments are not generally taken seriously by other anthropologists or sociologists, who consider it to be either mistaken in its facts, or mistaken in its overall mission to do history as science. *Guns, Germs, and Steel* did, however, help to popularize the comparative method* in history.

Diamond's current work with development economists, looking at shorter time-scales and more specific problems, continues to be important. "What is going to happen in the United States?" Diamond asks in a recent article, in the context of declining global prominence and mounting budgetary pressure.[1]

Having restated his argument that China slipped behind the West because of its political unity, he suggests that political competition moves ideas and development forward, while allowing bad ideas (the abolition of the navy, for example, or the destruction of the middle

> ❝ Both long-termers and short-termers agree that the West has dominated the globe for the last two hundred years, but disagree over what the world was like before this. Everything revolves around their differing assumptions of premodern history. The only way we can resolve this dispute is by looking at these earlier periods to establish the overall 'shape' of history. ❞
>
> Ian Morris, *Why the West Rules—For Now*

class) to fail.[2]

Diamond notes four threats to this good state of affairs: political compromise has been declining; there are increasing restrictions on the right to vote; there is a growing gap between the rich and the poor; and, finally, there are too few opportunities to develop intellectual capital*[3] (that is, the nation's wealth of ideas, technology, and innovation). Diamond concludes this means the US will slowly lose the competitive advantages it has accumulated.

Future Directions

Diamond has written increasingly about culture (*The World Until Yesterday*) and methodology (*Natural Experiments of History*). The classical historian Ian Morris, however, has written two books recently that push the *Guns, Germs, and Steel* hypothesis forward.

His book *Why the West Rules—For Now: The Patterns of History and What They Reveal About the Future* (2010) attempts to bridge the gap between long- and short-term approaches to global history. "We will not find answers," Morris writes, "if we restrict our search to prehistory or modern times." Instead, historians ought to "look at the whole sweep of human history as a single story, establishing its overall shape."[4] Whereas Diamond argues that only the very earliest factors matter as causes (everything else is just a knock-on effect), Morris believes "ultimate" causes can emerge throughout history: "Western rule was neither predetermined thousands of years ago nor a result of recent accidents."[5]

The key concept of Morris's work is "social development," which he takes to mean "a group's ability to master its physical and intellectual environment to 'get things done' ... the bundle of technological, subsistence, organizational, and cultural accomplishments" through which people understand and manage the natural and social worlds.[6]

Morris concludes that geography and "social development" determine the shape of history, and constantly redefine one another, writing that "geography determined where in the world social development would rise fastest, but rising social development changes what geography meant."[7] Britain may have lost out on the spread of technology that occurred in Europe after the medieval period, for example, being an island off the continent, but when having powerful navies became important for global domination, then Britain's position on the Atlantic was a major advantage in developing its empire.

Summary

Jared Diamond's *Guns, Germs, and Steel* was both a timely and a controversial book. He aimed to present a view of history that went beyond simple, obvious explanations of why the world is the way it is—and particularly why "the West" is so powerful. He dismisses answers that look only at the obvious, "proximate" causes, which would explain Western domination by its superior technology or singular forms of government, because they tell only part of the story. He prefers to dig deeper, looking for "ultimate" causes: If technology is key to dominating the world, why, then, did the West develop better technology?

To make his arguments, Diamond looks to archaeology to examine the first divergences between groups that would become the complex societies in which technology develops and those societies that remains as hunter-gatherers,* where complex technology does not develop. The key difference was *agriculture*. Societies that become agricultural can have specialist rulers, scientists, blacksmiths, and scribes. Looking for ultimate causes, Diamond goes back a step further: why do some societies develop agriculture, and others do not? Random geographical factors determine the presence of plants and animals that are well suited to domestication.* For Diamond, this inevitably led to agriculture, which led to society, which led to "guns, germs, and steel"—and eventually Western global dominance.

NOTES

1   Jared Diamond, "Four Threats to American Democracy," *Governance* 27, no. 2 (2014): 189.

2   Diamond, "Four Threats to American Democracy," 186.

3   Diamond, "Four Threats to American Democracy," 186–7.

4   Ian Morris, *Why the West Rules—For Now: The Patterns of History and What They Reveal About the Future* (New York: Farrar, Straus and Giroux, 2010), 22.

5   Morris, *Why The West Rules*, 25.

6   Morris, *Why The West Rules*, 144.

7   Morris, *Why The West Rules*, 35.

GLOSSARY

GLOSSARY OF TERMS

Annales school: a historical school of thought that emphasizes the long-term influences on day-to-day living, rather than dramatic events.

Cajamarca: a major city in Peru. It was also the site of a major battle between Spanish conquistadors and native Incas.

Capitalism: an economic system in which most industrial activity (but not necessarily all) is controlled by private owners, for profit.

Cold War (1947–91): a period of tension between the United States and the Soviet Union, and their allies. While the two blocs never engaged in direct military conflict, they engaged in covert and proxy wars and espionage.

Colonialism: the invasion and establishment of a colony in a target territory by a central state. It is characterized by a deeply unequal relationship between the native and colonizing populations.

Comparative method: involves examining two cases and identifying the underlying factors that have driven their respective outcomes.

Conquistadors: a term used to describe Spanish and Portuguese explorers and soldiers who simultaneously "discovered" and conquered lands in the Americas, Oceania, and even parts of Asia, especially between the fifteenth and seventeenth centuries.

Despotism: a form of government that invests all authority in one individual or group of individuals.

Domestication: refers to the process by which humans use selective breeding in order to encourage or discourage certain traits that make the organism more useful.

Empiricism: a theory of knowledge. It holds that knowledge comes only from what one can observe.

Environmental determinism: the idea that factors in an environment "lock in" given historical trajectories. It is an extreme form of structuralism, because it has no space for agency (that is, the potential of individuals to change circumstances through action).

Eurocentrism: a criticism of many Western social scientific theories. The criticism is that these theories make many assumptions that Europeans would make, especially about the natural superiority of Europe and European ideas, which members of other cultures do not see as natural.

Globalization: the process of increasing interconnectedness around the globe, driven by improvements in travel, shipping, and telecommunications, among other technologies.

Hunter–gatherers: a small group of humans that relies on wild sources of food (hunting, rather than raising animals, and gathering, rather than farming, plants). Societies organized along these lines tend to move frequently and to devote much time to food procurement.

Ice Age: a reduction in the temperature of the Earth's surface over a long period of time. During an Ice Age, most of North America and Europe would be covered by glacier ice. The last Ice Age ended some 12,500 years ago.

Intellectual capital: roughly, the value of ideas, knowledge, and innovation.

Laboratory conditions: refers to the careful, controlled environment of a laboratory, where a phenomenon can be studied without interference from the outside world.

Longue durée: a French phrase meaning "long term," and referring, in the context of history, to the approach taken by the historians of the Annales school, concerned with historical changes (often social changes) over the long term.

Ludwig von Mises Institute: a think tank from the United States that promotes lower levels of government interference in daily life. It is named after Austrian economist Ludwig von Mises, who was skeptical of the government's ability to plan more effectively than the free market.

Malaria: a disease caused by a parasite carried in mosquitoes. It only appears in warm, wet areas of the world. Over 600,000 people died of malaria in 2010.

Man–land geography: one of the four major traditions of geography, emphasizing how the environment and people mutually affect one another.

Natural experiments: these occur, usually by luck, when two groups of individuals who are mostly similar are exposed to two different conditions. Researchers can infer what one condition does to one group, relative to another.

Natural selection: the process, first described by Charles Darwin, whereby some traits in organisms affect the reproductive success of that organism under given conditions, and those traits thereby become more or less prevalent.

Parsimony: refers to the principle that a theory should make predictions as simply as possible, using as few factors as necessary.

Processual archaeology: a school of thought in archaeology that suggests archaeology should seek to use physical evidence of the past in order to reconstruct what life was genuinely like. It aims to establish "laws" of human behavior based on commonalities between cultures.

Pulitzer Prize: a highly prestigious American award for excellence in newspaper and online journalism, as well as literature and musical composition.

Stone Age: refers to two separate, related things. It refers to an era of prehistory that was characterized by the use of stone tools by humans, ending between 6000 and 3000 B.C.E. It also refers to levels of technological development that still exist among some scattered hunter-gatherer tribes.

Structuralism: a way of seeing the world in social sciences that emphasizes the causal role of external conditions in shaping human action. It is often opposed to agency, which emphasizes the causal role of individual motivation.

Subsidy: a form of financial support extended (usually by a government) to a sector of the economy, in order to make it more competitive.

Temperate climates: these exist between the warm tropical regions and the cold arctic regions of the Earth. Temperate climates are characterized by four seasons, with moderate temperatures.

Treaty of Versailles (1919): refers to the peace treaty signed between the Allied Powers and a defeated Germany at the end of World War I. It has historically been criticized for being too punitive on Germany, and contributing to the degradation of its already fragile economy.

Tropical climates: these tend to cluster near the equator and are characterized by year-round warmth.

Underdevelopment: a condition that is experienced by states that are not using their resources to their full productive potential.

Uneven development: refers to the process whereby different areas develop economically at different rates.

United Nations: a supra-governmental organization headquartered in New York City comprising nearly every state in the world. Its most important functions include overseeing global security matters and promoting global cooperation.

World Bank: an international institution based in Washington, DC. It offers loans and advice to countries that require development assistance.

World-systems theory: an approach to world sociology and history that turns on the idea that some countries are systematically exploited by others.

World Trade Organization: an international institution based in Geneva, Switzerland. It regulates trade between countries, and attempts to ensure it is fair and open.

World War II (1939–45): a global conflict fought between the Axis Powers (Germany, Italy, and Japan) and the victorious Allied Powers (United Kingdom and its colonies and dominions, the former Soviet Union, and the United States).

PEOPLE MENTIONED IN THE TEXT

Daron Acemoglu (b. 1967) is a Turkish American development economist. He and the economist James Robinson famously take an "institutions" approach to development, meaning states with "good" institutions (non-extractive, fair, and so on) will out-develop states with "bad" institutions.

Atahuallpa (1500–33) was an Incan emperor. Atahuallpa was captured by the Spanish in 1532, and was briefly imprisoned before being executed.

James Blaut (1927–2000) was professor of anthropology at the University of Illinois at Chicago. Blaut's career was characterized by the exposure of Eurocentric biases in mainstream history.

Fernand Braudel (1902–85) was a French historian, and key figure in the Annales school. He is notable for emphasizing the role of large-scale, long-term socio-economic shifts in driving history (rather than the decisions of kings).

Gene Callahan (b. 1959) is an American economist. Callahan argues in favor of reliance on the free market, rather than central planning.

William Catton (1929–2015) was an American sociologist. He is notable as one of the founders of environmental sociology, which was one of the first forms of sociology to look beyond purely social factors.

Christopher Columbus (1451–1506) was an Italian explorer. Looking for an alternative route to India, Columbus famously sailed from Europe, across the Atlantic, to America in 1492.

Alfred Crosby (b. 1931) is an American historian and geographer. He is famous for his book *The Colombian Exchange*, which explores the effect of the separation of Earth's two major landmasses coming to an abrupt halt in 1492 with the voyage of Columbus.

Charles Darwin (1809–82) was a British naturalist, famous for setting out the theory of evolution by natural selection.

Wade Davis (b. 1953) is a Canadian anthropologist and naturalist. His work emphasizes the differences between different cultures, and a rejection of any idea that one culture can be called superior to another.

Riley Dunlap is an American sociologist at Oklahoma State University. Along with William Catton, Dunlap is famous for setting out the environmental theory of sociology.

Frederick Errington is distinguished professor of anthropology at Trinity College, Connecticut. His work with Deborah Gewertz emphasizes themes of economics and culture, complex theories of change, and the importance of multiple perspectives in understanding all of the above.

John Gallup (b. 1962) is an American development economist. He has published numerous papers on the influence of different geographic factors on development outcomes.

Bill Gates (b. 1955) is an American entrepreneur and philanthropist, and has occupied the top of the world's rich list. He made his fortune founding Microsoft, but now supports economic development through the Bill and Melinda Gates Foundation.

Deborah Gewertz is professor of anthropology at Amherst College in Massachusetts. Her work with the anthropologist Frederick Errington emphasizes themes of economics and culture, complex theories of change, and the importance of multiple perspectives in understanding all of the above.

David Humphreys is a British professor of social policy at Green Templeton College at the University of Oxford.

Ellsworth Huntington (1876–1947) was an American geographer. He is known for his theory of geographic determinism.

Mark D. Jacobs is professor of sociology at George Mason University in the United States. Studying trends in the discipline of sociology is one of his key research interests, but he has also studied the sociology of finance.

Eric Jones (b. 1936) is a British Australian economic historian. His book *The European Miracle* sought to explain why industrial productivity was so high in Europe.

David Landes (1924–2013) was an American professor of economics and history at Harvard University.

Philip Mancus is professor of psychology and sociology at the College of the Redwoods in the United States. His work focuses on human behavior.

Patricia McAnany (b. 1963) is an American anthropologist who specializes in the history and archaeology of the Mayan civilization in the Americas.

Andrew Mellinger is an American economist who is known for his writing on the relation between development economics and geography.

Ian Morris (b. 1960) is an Anglo-American historian, specializing in classics. He specializes in long-term history, and his recent work focuses on the role of warfare in economic development.

Nathan Nunn is a Canadian professor of economics at Harvard University. He is well known for his work on economic history, especially with relation to development.

William D. Pattison (1921–97) was an American geographer at the University of Chicago. He is well known not only for his work on geography as a discipline, but also in patterns of land use in the United States.

Francisco Pizarro (c. 1471–1541) was a Spanish colonial commander. He commanded the forces that conquered the Incan empire. He became the first governor of the Spanish territories in what is now Peru in 1528.

James Robinson (b. 1960) is a British economist and political theorist at Harvard University. His work with Daron Acemoglu in development economics, *Why Nations Fail*, is known for emphasizing the role of policy and institutions.

Jeffrey Sachs (b. 1954) is an American economist at Harvard University. He focuses on sustainable development, especially regarding the environment. He was involved in the creation of the United Nations Millennium Development Goals.

Lyn Spillman is professor of sociology at the University of Notre Dame in the US. Her work examines the influence of social forces on political strategy.

Julien Steward (1902–72) was an American anthropologist. His research focused on the ways in which humanity manipulates our natural environment to sustain ourselves.

Paul Streeten (b. 1917) is an Anglo-Austrian American development economist. He was known for outlining the "basic needs" approach to development, and advising the British Ministry of Overseas Development in the 1960s.

Stuart Vyse is professor of psychology at Connecticut College. He specializes in the analysis of behavior.

Immanuel Wallerstein (b. 1930) is an American sociologist, best known for promoting world-systems theory. The theory states that there is a division of labor between the developed "core" states (the West, primarily) and peripheral states. The core uses the periphery to extract resources and labor for its own benefit.

Andrew Warner is an American economist. He is concerned with theorizing how and why governments invest in their own development.

Stephen Wertheim is a young American historian. He wrote his review of Diamond in the journal *Nation* while still a graduate student at Columbia University.

Michael Wilcox is an associate professor of anthropology at Stanford University in the US. His research interests focus on the history of the native populations of the Southwestern United States.

Yali (1912–75) was a Papua New Guinean politician and activist. His political career involved mediating relationships between the central government and the native communities.

Norman Yoffee is professor of anthropology and Near Eastern studies at New York University. He is particularly interested in ancient Mesopotamia, and what factors prompted ancient states to rise and fall.

Richard York is professor of sociology and environmental studies at the University of Oregon. His work focuses on climate change and human impact on the environment.

WORKS CITED

WORKS CITED

Acemoglu, Daron, and James Robinson. *Why Nations Fail: The Origins of Power, Prosperity, and Poverty*. London: Profile Books, 2012.

Blaut, James. "Environmentalism and Eurocentrism." *Geographical Review* 89, no. 3 (1999): 391–408.

Braudel, Fernand. *The Mediterranean World in the Age of Philip II: Volume I*. London: University of California Press, 1995.

Callahan, Gene. "The Diamond Fallacy," Mises Institute. Accessed May 17, 2015. https://mises.org/library/diamond-fallacy.

Crosby, Alfred W. *The Colombian Exchange: Biological and Cultural Consequences of 1492*. Westport, CT: Praeger, 2003.

Darwin, Charles. *On the Origin of Species*. Oxford: Oxford University Press, 2008.

Davis, Wade. "The World Until Yesterday by Jared Diamond: A Review." *Guardian*, January 9, 2013. Accessed May 23, 2015. http://www.theguardian.com/books/2013/jan/09/history-society.

Diamond, Jared. "Guns, Germs, and Steel." *New York Review of Books*, June 26, 1997. Accessed May 23, 2015. http://www.nybooks.com/articles/archives/1997/jun/26/guns-germs-and-steel/

— — —. *Guns, Germs, and Steel: The Fates of Human Societies*. New York: W. W. Norton & Company, 1999.

— — —. *The Rise and Fall of the Third Chimpanzee*. London: Vintage, 2002.

— — —. *Collapse: How Societies Choose to Fail or Survive*. London: Penguin, 2005.

— — —. "Guns, Germs, and Steel: The Fates of Human Societies." Accessed September 6, 2013. http://www.jareddiamond.org/Jared_Diamond/Guns,_Germs,_and_Steel.html.

— — —. *The World Until Yesterday: What Can We Learn from Traditional Societies?* London: Penguin, 2013.

— — —. "Four Threats to American Democracy." *Governance* 27, no. 2 (2014): 185–9.

— — —. "About Me." Accessed May 30, 2015. http://www.jareddiamond.org/Jared_Diamond/About_Me.html.

Diamond, Jared, and James Robinson. "Afterword." In *Natural Experiments of History*, edited by Jared Diamond and James Robinson, 142–75. Cambridge, MA: Harvard University Press, 2010.

Dunlap, Riley, and William Catton. "Environmental Sociology." *Annual Review of Sociology* 5 (1979): 243–73.

Earle, Timothy K., and Robert W. Preucel. "Processual Archaeology and the Radical Critique." *Current Anthropology* 28, no. 4 (1987): 501–38.

Errington, Frederick, and Deborah Gewertz. *Yali's Question: Sugar, Culture, and History*. Chicago: University of Chicago Press, 2004.

— — —. "Excusing the Haves and Blaming the Have Nots in the Telling of History." In *Questioning Collapse: Human Resilience, Ecological Vulnerability, and the Aftermath of Empire*, edited by Patricia McAnany and Norman Yoffee, 329–51. Cambridge: Cambridge University Press, 2009.

Gallup, John, Jeffrey Sachs, and Andrew Mellinger. *Geography and Economic Development*. Cambridge: National Bureau of Economic Research, 1998.

Hickey, Maureen, and Vicky Lawson. "Beyond Science? Human Geography, Interpretation, and Critique." In *Questioning Geography: Fundamental Debates*, edited by Noel Castree, Alisdair Rogers, and Douglas Sherman, 96–115. Malden, MA: Blackwell, 2005.

Hippocrates. *On Airs, Waters, and Places*. Translated by Francis Adams. Accessed May 2, 2015. http://classics.mit.edu/Hippocrates/airwatpl.1.1.html.

Humphreys, David K., Manuel P. Eisner, and Douglas J. Wiebe. "Evaluating the Impact of Flexible Alcohol Trading Hours on Violence: An Interrupted Time Series Analysis." *PLOS ONE* 8, no. 2 (2013). Accessed July 15, 2015. doi:10.1371/journal.pone.0055581.

Huntington, Ellsworth. *Civilization and Climate*. New Haven, CT: Yale University Press, 1915.

Jacobs, Mark D., and Lyn Spillman. "Cultural Sociology at the Crossroads of a Discipline." *Poetics* 33 (2005): 1–14.

Jones, Eric. *The European Miracle: Environments, Economies, and Geopolitics in the History of Europe and Asia*. Cambridge: Cambridge University Press, 2003.

Landes, David. *The Wealth and Poverty of Nations: Why Some Are So Rich and Some Are So Poor*. New York: W. W. Norton & Company, 1998.

McKie, Robin. "Jared Diamond: What We Can Learn from Tribal Life." *Guardian*, January 6, 2013. Accessed July 15, 2015. http://www.theguardian.com/science/2013/jan/06/jared-diamond-tribal-life-anthropology.

Miller, Christopher. "Review of *Guns, Germs, and Steel: The Fate of Human Societies*, by Jared Diamond." *Economic Botany* 56, no. 2 (2002): 209.

Mock, Gregory, ed. *A Guide to World Resources 2005*. Washington, DC: World Resources Institute, 2005.

Morris, Ian. *Why the West Rules—For Now: The Patterns of History and What They Reveal About the Future*. New York: Farrar, Straus and Giroux, 2010.

Nunn, Nathan. "Shackled to the Past: The Causes and Consequences of Africa's Slave Trades." In *Natural Experiments of History*, edited by Jared Diamond and James Robinson, 142–84. Cambridge, MA: Harvard University Press, 2010.

Pattison, William. "The Four Traditions of Geography." *Journal of Geography* 63, no. 5 (1964): 211–16.

Sachs, Jeffrey. "Institutions Matter, but Not for Everything." *Finance and Development* 40, no. 2 (June 2003): 38–41.

Sachs Jeffrey, and Andrew Warner. "The Curse of Natural Resources." *European Economic Review* 45, nos. 4–6 (2001): 827–38.

Sluyter, Andrew. "Neo-Environmental Determinism, Intellectual Damage Control, and Nature/Society Science." *Antipode* 35, no. 4 (2003): 813–17.

Steward, Julien. *Theory of Culture Change: The Methodology of Multilinear Evolution*. Chicago: University of Illinois Press, 1972.

Streeten, Paul. "How Poor Are the Poor Countries?" In *Development in a Divided World*, edited by D. Seers and L. Joy, 67–83. Harmondsworth: Penguin, 1971.

ul-Haq, Mahbub, ed. *Human Development Report 1990*. New York: Oxford University Press, 1990.

Vyse, Stuart. "World History for Behavior Analysts: Jared Diamond's *Guns, Germs, and Steel*." *Behavior and Social Issues* 11, no. 1 (2001): 80–7.

Wallerstein, Immanuel. *The Modern World System I: Capitalist Agriculture and the Origins of the European World Economy in the Sixteenth Century*. London: University of California Press, 2011.

Wertheim, Stephen. "Hunter-Blatherer." *The Nation*, April 22, 2013.

Wilcox, Michael. *The Pueblo Revolt and the Mythology of Conquest: An Indigenous Archaeology*. Berkeley, CA: University of California Press, 2009.

———. "Marketing Conquest and the Vanishing Indian: An Indigenous Response to Jared Diamond's *Guns, Germs, and Steel*." *Journal of Social Archaeology* 10, no. 1 (2010): 92–117.

York, Richard, and Philip Mancus. "Diamond in the Rough: Reflections on *Guns, Germs, and Steel*." *Research in Human Ecology* 14, no. 2 (2007): 157–62.

THE MACAT LIBRARY
BY DISCIPLINE

AFRICANA STUDIES

Chinua Achebe's *An Image of Africa: Racism in Conrad's Heart of Darkness*
W. E. B. Du Bois's *The Souls of Black Folk*
Zora Neale Huston's *Characteristics of Negro Expression*
Martin Luther King Jr's *Why We Can't Wait*
Toni Morrison's *Playing in the Dark: Whiteness in the American Literary Imagination*

ANTHROPOLOGY

Arjun Appadurai's *Modernity at Large: Cultural Dimensions of Globalisation*
Philippe Ariès's *Centuries of Childhood*
Franz Boas's *Race, Language and Culture*
Kim Chan & Renée Mauborgne's *Blue Ocean Strategy*
Jared Diamond's *Guns, Germs & Steel: the Fate of Human Societies*
Jared Diamond's *Collapse: How Societies Choose to Fail or Survive*
E. E. Evans-Pritchard's *Witchcraft, Oracles and Magic Among the Azande*
James Ferguson's *The Anti-Politics Machine*
Clifford Geertz's *The Interpretation of Cultures*
David Graeber's *Debt: the First 5000 Years*
Karen Ho's *Liquidated: An Ethnography of Wall Street*
Geert Hofstede's *Culture's Consequences: Comparing Values, Behaviors, Institutes and Organizations across Nations*
Claude Lévi-Strauss's *Structural Anthropology*
Jay Macleod's *Ain't No Makin' It: Aspirations and Attainment in a Low-Income Neighborhood*
Saba Mahmood's *The Politics of Piety: The Islamic Revival and the Feminist Subject*
Marcel Mauss's *The Gift*

BUSINESS

Jean Lave & Etienne Wenger's *Situated Learning*
Theodore Levitt's *Marketing Myopia*
Burton G. Malkiel's *A Random Walk Down Wall Street*
Douglas McGregor's *The Human Side of Enterprise*
Michael Porter's *Competitive Strategy: Creating and Sustaining Superior Performance*
John Kotter's *Leading Change*
C. K. Prahalad & Gary Hamel's *The Core Competence of the Corporation*

CRIMINOLOGY

Michelle Alexander's *The New Jim Crow: Mass Incarceration in the Age of Colorblindness*
Michael R. Gottfredson & Travis Hirschi's *A General Theory of Crime*
Richard Herrnstein & Charles A. Murray's *The Bell Curve: Intelligence and Class Structure in American Life*
Elizabeth Loftus's *Eyewitness Testimony*
Jay Macleod's *Ain't No Makin' It: Aspirations and Attainment in a Low-Income Neighborhood*
Philip Zimbardo's *The Lucifer Effect*

ECONOMICS

Janet Abu-Lughod's *Before European Hegemony*
Ha-Joon Chang's *Kicking Away the Ladder*
David Brion Davis's *The Problem of Slavery in the Age of Revolution*
Milton Friedman's *The Role of Monetary Policy*
Milton Friedman's *Capitalism and Freedom*
David Graeber's *Debt: the First 5000 Years*
Friedrich Hayek's *The Road to Serfdom*
Karen Ho's *Liquidated: An Ethnography of Wall Street*

John Maynard Keynes's *The General Theory of Employment, Interest and Money*
Charles P. Kindleberger's *Manias, Panics and Crashes*
Robert Lucas's *Why Doesn't Capital Flow from Rich to Poor Countries?*
Burton G. Malkiel's *A Random Walk Down Wall Street*
Thomas Robert Malthus's *An Essay on the Principle of Population*
Karl Marx's *Capital*
Thomas Piketty's *Capital in the Twenty-First Century*
Amartya Sen's *Development as Freedom*
Adam Smith's *The Wealth of Nations*
Nassim Nicholas Taleb's *The Black Swan: The Impact of the Highly Improbable*
Amos Tversky's & Daniel Kahneman's *Judgment under Uncertainty: Heuristics and Biases*
Mahbub Ul Haq's *Reflections on Human Development*
Max Weber's *The Protestant Ethic and the Spirit of Capitalism*

FEMINISM AND GENDER STUDIES

Judith Butler's *Gender Trouble*
Simone De Beauvoir's *The Second Sex*
Michel Foucault's *History of Sexuality*
Betty Friedan's *The Feminine Mystique*
Saba Mahmood's *The Politics of Piety: The Islamic Revival and the Feminist Subject*
Joan Wallach Scott's *Gender and the Politics of History*
Mary Wollstonecraft's *A Vindication of the Rights of Woman*
Virginia Woolf's *A Room of One's Own*

GEOGRAPHY

The Brundtland Report's *Our Common Future*
Rachel Carson's *Silent Spring*
Charles Darwin's *On the Origin of Species*
James Ferguson's *The Anti-Politics Machine*
Jane Jacobs's *The Death and Life of Great American Cities*
James Lovelock's *Gaia: A New Look at Life on Earth*
Amartya Sen's *Development as Freedom*
Mathis Wackernagel & William Rees's *Our Ecological Footprint*

HISTORY

Janet Abu-Lughod's *Before European Hegemony*
Benedict Anderson's *Imagined Communities*
Bernard Bailyn's *The Ideological Origins of the American Revolution*
Hanna Batatu's *The Old Social Classes And The Revolutionary Movements Of Iraq*
Christopher Browning's *Ordinary Men: Reserve Police Batallion 101 and the Final Solution in Poland*
Edmund Burke's *Reflections on the Revolution in France*
William Cronon's *Nature's Metropolis: Chicago And The Great West*
Alfred W. Crosby's *The Columbian Exchange*
Hamid Dabashi's *Iran: A People Interrupted*
David Brion Davis's *The Problem of Slavery in the Age of Revolution*
Nathalie Zemon Davis's *The Return of Martin Guerre*
Jared Diamond's *Guns, Germs & Steel: the Fate of Human Societies*
Frank Dikotter's *Mao's Great Famine*
John W Dower's *War Without Mercy: Race And Power In The Pacific War*
W. E. B. Du Bois's *The Souls of Black Folk*
Richard J. Evans's *In Defence of History*
Lucien Febvre's *The Problem of Unbelief in the 16th Century*
Sheila Fitzpatrick's *Everyday Stalinism*

Eric Foner's *Reconstruction: America's Unfinished Revolution, 1863-1877*
Michel Foucault's *Discipline and Punish*
Michel Foucault's *History of Sexuality*
Francis Fukuyama's *The End of History and the Last Man*
John Lewis Gaddis's *We Now Know: Rethinking Cold War History*
Ernest Gellner's *Nations and Nationalism*
Eugene Genovese's *Roll, Jordan, Roll: The World the Slaves Made*
Carlo Ginzburg's *The Night Battles*
Daniel Goldhagen's *Hitler's Willing Executioners*
Jack Goldstone's *Revolution and Rebellion in the Early Modern World*
Antonio Gramsci's *The Prison Notebooks*
Alexander Hamilton, John Jay & James Madison's *The Federalist Papers*
Christopher Hill's *The World Turned Upside Down*
Carole Hillenbrand's *The Crusades: Islamic Perspectives*
Thomas Hobbes's *Leviathan*
Eric Hobsbawm's *The Age Of Revolution*
John A. Hobson's *Imperialism: A Study*
Albert Hourani's *History of the Arab Peoples*
Samuel P. Huntington's *The Clash of Civilizations and the Remaking of World Order*
C. L. R. James's *The Black Jacobins*
Tony Judt's *Postwar: A History of Europe Since 1945*
Ernst Kantorowicz's *The King's Two Bodies: A Study in Medieval Political Theology*
Paul Kennedy's *The Rise and Fall of the Great Powers*
Ian Kershaw's *The "Hitler Myth": Image and Reality in the Third Reich*
John Maynard Keynes's *The General Theory of Employment, Interest and Money*
Charles P. Kindleberger's *Manias, Panics and Crashes*
Martin Luther King Jr's *Why We Can't Wait*
Henry Kissinger's *World Order: Reflections on the Character of Nations and the Course of History*
Thomas Kuhn's *The Structure of Scientific Revolutions*
Georges Lefebvre's *The Coming of the French Revolution*
John Locke's *Two Treatises of Government*
Niccolò Machiavelli's *The Prince*
Thomas Robert Malthus's *An Essay on the Principle of Population*
Mahmood Mamdani's *Citizen and Subject: Contemporary Africa And The Legacy Of Late Colonialism*
Karl Marx's *Capital*
Stanley Milgram's *Obedience to Authority*
John Stuart Mill's *On Liberty*
Thomas Paine's *Common Sense*
Thomas Paine's *Rights of Man*
Geoffrey Parker's *Global Crisis: War, Climate Change and Catastrophe in the Seventeenth Century*
Jonathan Riley-Smith's *The First Crusade and the Idea of Crusading*
Jean-Jacques Rousseau's *The Social Contract*
Joan Wallach Scott's *Gender and the Politics of History*
Theda Skocpol's *States and Social Revolutions*
Adam Smith's *The Wealth of Nations*
Timothy Snyder's *Bloodlands: Europe Between Hitler and Stalin*
Sun Tzu's *The Art of War*
Keith Thomas's *Religion and the Decline of Magic*
Thucydides's *The History of the Peloponnesian War*
Frederick Jackson Turner's *The Significance of the Frontier in American History*
Odd Arne Westad's *The Global Cold War: Third World Interventions And The Making Of Our Times*

LITERATURE

Chinua Achebe's *An Image of Africa: Racism in Conrad's Heart of Darkness*
Roland Barthes's *Mythologies*
Homi K. Bhabha's *The Location of Culture*
Judith Butler's *Gender Trouble*
Simone De Beauvoir's *The Second Sex*
Ferdinand De Saussure's *Course in General Linguistics*
T. S. Eliot's *The Sacred Wood: Essays on Poetry and Criticism*
Zora Neale Huston's *Characteristics of Negro Expression*
Toni Morrison's *Playing in the Dark: Whiteness in the American Literary Imagination*
Edward Said's *Orientalism*
Gayatri Chakravorty Spivak's *Can the Subaltern Speak?*
Mary Wollstonecraft's *A Vindication of the Rights of Women*
Virginia Woolf's *A Room of One's Own*

PHILOSOPHY

Elizabeth Anscombe's *Modern Moral Philosophy*
Hannah Arendt's *The Human Condition*
Aristotle's *Metaphysics*
Aristotle's *Nicomachean Ethics*
Edmund Gettier's *Is Justified True Belief Knowledge?*
Georg Wilhelm Friedrich Hegel's *Phenomenology of Spirit*
David Hume's *Dialogues Concerning Natural Religion*
David Hume's *The Enquiry for Human Understanding*
Immanuel Kant's *Religion within the Boundaries of Mere Reason*
Immanuel Kant's *Critique of Pure Reason*
Søren Kierkegaard's *The Sickness Unto Death*
Søren Kierkegaard's *Fear and Trembling*
C. S. Lewis's *The Abolition of Man*
Alasdair MacIntyre's *After Virtue*
Marcus Aurelius's *Meditations*
Friedrich Nietzsche's *On the Genealogy of Morality*
Friedrich Nietzsche's *Beyond Good and Evil*
Plato's *Republic*
Plato's *Symposium*
Jean-Jacques Rousseau's *The Social Contract*
Gilbert Ryle's *The Concept of Mind*
Baruch Spinoza's *Ethics*
Sun Tzu's *The Art of War*
Ludwig Wittgenstein's *Philosophical Investigations*

POLITICS

Benedict Anderson's *Imagined Communities*
Aristotle's *Politics*
Bernard Bailyn's *The Ideological Origins of the American Revolution*
Edmund Burke's *Reflections on the Revolution in France*
John C. Calhoun's *A Disquisition on Government*
Ha-Joon Chang's *Kicking Away the Ladder*
Hamid Dabashi's *Iran: A People Interrupted*
Hamid Dabashi's *Theology of Discontent: The Ideological Foundation of the Islamic Revolution in Iran*
Robert Dahl's *Democracy and its Critics*
Robert Dahl's *Who Governs?*
David Brion Davis's *The Problem of Slavery in the Age of Revolution*

Alexis De Tocqueville's *Democracy in America*
James Ferguson's *The Anti-Politics Machine*
Frank Dikotter's *Mao's Great Famine*
Sheila Fitzpatrick's *Everyday Stalinism*
Eric Foner's *Reconstruction: America's Unfinished Revolution, 1863-1877*
Milton Friedman's *Capitalism and Freedom*
Francis Fukuyama's *The End of History and the Last Man*
John Lewis Gaddis's *We Now Know: Rethinking Cold War History*
Ernest Gellner's *Nations and Nationalism*
David Graeber's *Debt: the First 5000 Years*
Antonio Gramsci's *The Prison Notebooks*
Alexander Hamilton, John Jay & James Madison's *The Federalist Papers*
Friedrich Hayek's *The Road to Serfdom*
Christopher Hill's *The World Turned Upside Down*
Thomas Hobbes's *Leviathan*
John A. Hobson's *Imperialism: A Study*
Samuel P. Huntington's *The Clash of Civilizations and the Remaking of World Order*
Tony Judt's *Postwar: A History of Europe Since 1945*
David C. Kang's *China Rising: Peace, Power and Order in East Asia*
Paul Kennedy's *The Rise and Fall of Great Powers*
Robert Keohane's *After Hegemony*
Martin Luther King Jr.'s *Why We Can't Wait*
Henry Kissinger's *World Order: Reflections on the Character of Nations and the Course of History*
John Locke's *Two Treatises of Government*
Niccolò Machiavelli's *The Prince*
Thomas Robert Malthus's *An Essay on the Principle of Population*
Mahmood Mamdani's *Citizen and Subject: Contemporary Africa And The Legacy Of Late Colonialism*
Karl Marx's *Capital*
John Stuart Mill's *On Liberty*
John Stuart Mill's *Utilitarianism*
Hans Morgenthau's *Politics Among Nations*
Thomas Paine's *Common Sense*
Thomas Paine's *Rights of Man*
Thomas Piketty's *Capital in the Twenty-First Century*
Robert D. Putman's *Bowling Alone*
John Rawls's *Theory of Justice*
Jean-Jacques Rousseau's *The Social Contract*
Theda Skocpol's *States and Social Revolutions*
Adam Smith's *The Wealth of Nations*
Sun Tzu's *The Art of War*
Henry David Thoreau's *Civil Disobedience*
Thucydides's *The History of the Peloponnesian War*
Kenneth Waltz's *Theory of International Politics*
Max Weber's *Politics as a Vocation*
Odd Arne Westad's *The Global Cold War: Third World Interventions And The Making Of Our Times*

POSTCOLONIAL STUDIES

Roland Barthes's *Mythologies*
Frantz Fanon's *Black Skin, White Masks*
Homi K. Bhabha's *The Location of Culture*
Gustavo Gutiérrez's *A Theology of Liberation*
Edward Said's *Orientalism*
Gayatri Chakravorty Spivak's *Can the Subaltern Speak?*

PSYCHOLOGY

Gordon Allport's *The Nature of Prejudice*
Alan Baddeley & Graham Hitch's *Aggression: A Social Learning Analysis*
Albert Bandura's *Aggression: A Social Learning Analysis*
Leon Festinger's *A Theory of Cognitive Dissonance*
Sigmund Freud's *The Interpretation of Dreams*
Betty Friedan's *The Feminine Mystique*
Michael R. Gottfredson & Travis Hirschi's *A General Theory of Crime*
Eric Hoffer's *The True Believer: Thoughts on the Nature of Mass Movements*
William James's *Principles of Psychology*
Elizabeth Loftus's *Eyewitness Testimony*
A. H. Maslow's *A Theory of Human Motivation*
Stanley Milgram's *Obedience to Authority*
Steven Pinker's *The Better Angels of Our Nature*
Oliver Sacks's *The Man Who Mistook His Wife For a Hat*
Richard Thaler & Cass Sunstein's *Nudge: Improving Decisions About Health, Wealth and Happiness*
Amos Tversky's *Judgment under Uncertainty: Heuristics and Biases*
Philip Zimbardo's *The Lucifer Effect*

SCIENCE

Rachel Carson's *Silent Spring*
William Cronon's *Nature's Metropolis: Chicago And The Great West*
Alfred W. Crosby's *The Columbian Exchange*
Charles Darwin's *On the Origin of Species*
Richard Dawkin's *The Selfish Gene*
Thomas Kuhn's *The Structure of Scientific Revolutions*
Geoffrey Parker's *Global Crisis: War, Climate Change and Catastrophe in the Seventeenth Century*
Mathis Wackernagel & William Rees's *Our Ecological Footprint*

SOCIOLOGY

Michelle Alexander's *The New Jim Crow: Mass Incarceration in the Age of Colorblindness*
Gordon Allport's *The Nature of Prejudice*
Albert Bandura's *Aggression: A Social Learning Analysis*
Hanna Batatu's *The Old Social Classes And The Revolutionary Movements Of Iraq*
Ha-Joon Chang's *Kicking Away the Ladder*
W. E. B. Du Bois's *The Souls of Black Folk*
Émile Durkheim's *On Suicide*
Frantz Fanon's *Black Skin, White Masks*
Frantz Fanon's *The Wretched of the Earth*
Eric Foner's *Reconstruction: America's Unfinished Revolution, 1863-1877*
Eugene Genovese's *Roll, Jordan, Roll: The World the Slaves Made*
Jack Goldstone's *Revolution and Rebellion in the Early Modern World*
Antonio Gramsci's *The Prison Notebooks*
Richard Herrnstein & Charles A Murray's *The Bell Curve: Intelligence and Class Structure in American Life*
Eric Hoffer's *The True Believer: Thoughts on the Nature of Mass Movements*
Jane Jacobs's *The Death and Life of Great American Cities*
Robert Lucas's *Why Doesn't Capital Flow from Rich to Poor Countries?*
Jay Macleod's *Ain't No Makin' It: Aspirations and Attainment in a Low Income Neighborhood*
Elaine May's *Homeward Bound: American Families in the Cold War Era*
Douglas McGregor's *The Human Side of Enterprise*
C. Wright Mills's *The Sociological Imagination*

Thomas Piketty's *Capital in the Twenty-First Century*
Robert D. Putman's *Bowling Alone*
David Riesman's *The Lonely Crowd: A Study of the Changing American Character*
Edward Said's *Orientalism*
Joan Wallach Scott's *Gender and the Politics of History*
Theda Skocpol's *States and Social Revolutions*
Max Weber's *The Protestant Ethic and the Spirit of Capitalism*

THEOLOGY

Augustine's *Confessions*
Benedict's *Rule of St Benedict*
Gustavo Gutiérrez's *A Theology of Liberation*
Carole Hillenbrand's *The Crusades: Islamic Perspectives*
David Hume's *Dialogues Concerning Natural Religion*
Immanuel Kant's *Religion within the Boundaries of Mere Reason*
Ernst Kantorowicz's *The King's Two Bodies: A Study in Medieval Political Theology*
Søren Kierkegaard's *The Sickness Unto Death*
C. S. Lewis's *The Abolition of Man*
Saba Mahmood's *The Politics of Piety: The Islamic Revival and the Feminist Subject*
Baruch Spinoza's *Ethics*
Keith Thomas's *Religion and the Decline of Magic*

COMING SOON

Chris Argyris's *The Individual and the Organisation*
Seyla Benhabib's *The Rights of Others*
Walter Benjamin's *The Work Of Art in the Age of Mechanical Reproduction*
John Berger's *Ways of Seeing*
Pierre Bourdieu's *Outline of a Theory of Practice*
Mary Douglas's *Purity and Danger*
Roland Dworkin's *Taking Rights Seriously*
James G. March's *Exploration and Exploitation in Organisational Learning*
Ikujiro Nonaka's *A Dynamic Theory of Organizational Knowledge Creation*
Griselda Pollock's *Vision and Difference*
Amartya Sen's *Inequality Re-Examined*
Susan Sontag's *On Photography*
Yasser Tabbaa's *The Transformation of Islamic Art*
Ludwig von Mises's *Theory of Money and Credit*

Macat Disciplines

Access the greatest ideas and thinkers across entire disciplines, including

AFRICANA STUDIES

Chinua Achebe's *An Image of Africa: Racism in Conrad's Heart of Darkness*

W. E. B. Du Bois's *The Souls of Black Folk*

Zora Neale Hurston's *Characteristics of Negro Expression*

Martin Luther King Jr.'s *Why We Can't Wait*

Toni Morrison's *Playing in the Dark: Whiteness in the American Literary Imagination*

Macat Disciplines

Access the greatest ideas and thinkers across entire disciplines, including

FEMINISM, GENDER AND QUEER STUDIES

Simone De Beauvoir's
The Second Sex

Michel Foucault's
History of Sexuality

Betty Friedan's
The Feminine Mystique

Saba Mahmood's
*The Politics of Piety:
The Islamic Revival and
the Feminist Subject*

Joan Wallach Scott's
*Gender and the
Politics of History*

Mary Wollstonecraft's
*A Vindication of the
Rights of Woman*

Virginia Woolf's
A Room of One's Own

Judith Butler's
Gender Trouble

Macat analyses are available from all good bookshops and libraries.

Access hundreds of analyses through one, multimedia tool.
Join free for one month **library.macat.com**

Macat Disciplines

Access the greatest ideas and thinkers across entire disciplines, including

INEQUALITY

Ha-Joon Chang's, *Kicking Away the Ladder*

David Graeber's, *Debt: The First 5000 Years*

Robert E. Lucas's, *Why Doesn't Capital Flow from Rich To Poor Countries?*

Thomas Piketty's, *Capital in the Twenty-First Century*

Amartya Sen's, *Inequality Re-Examined*

Mahbub Ul Haq's, *Reflections on Human Development*

Macat analyses are available from all good bookshops and libraries.

Access hundreds of analyses through one, multimedia tool.

Join free for one month **library.macat.com**

Macat Disciplines

Access the greatest ideas and thinkers across entire disciplines, including

CRIMINOLOGY

Michelle Alexander's
The New Jim Crow:
Mass Incarceration in the
Age of Colorblindness

Michael R. Gottfredson
& Travis Hirschi's
A General Theory of Crime

Elizabeth Loftus's
Eyewitness Testimony

Richard Herrnstein
& Charles A. Murray's
The Bell Curve: Intelligence and
Class Structure in American Life

Jay Macleod's
Ain't No Makin' It:
Aspirations and Attainment in a
Low-Income Neighborhood

Philip Zimbardo's
The Lucifer Effect

Macat analyses are available from all good bookshops and libraries.

Access hundreds of analyses through one, multimedia tool.
Join free for one month **library.macat.com**

Macat Disciplines

Access the greatest ideas and thinkers across entire disciplines, including

Postcolonial Studies

Roland Barthes's *Mythologies*
Frantz Fanon's *Black Skin, White Masks*
Homi K. Bhabha's *The Location of Culture*
Gustavo Gutiérrez's *A Theology of Liberation*
Edward Said's *Orientalism*
Gayatri Chakravorty Spivak's *Can the Subaltern Speak?*

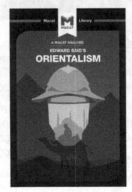

Macat Pairs

*Analyse historical and modern issues
from opposite sides of an argument.
Pairs include:*

HOW TO RUN AN ECONOMY

John Maynard Keynes's
*The General Theory OF Employment,
Interest and Money*

Classical economics suggests that market economies
are self-correcting in times of recession or depression,
and tend toward full employment and output. But
English economist John Maynard Keynes disagrees.

In his ground-breaking 1936 study *The General
Theory*, Keynes argues that traditional economics
has misunderstood the causes of unemployment.
Employment is not determined by the price of labor;
it is directly linked to demand. Keynes believes market
economies are by nature unstable, and so require
government intervention. Spurred on by the social
catastrophe of the Great Depression of the 1930s,
he sets out to revolutionize the way the world thinks

Milton Friedman's
The Role of Monetary Policy

Friedman's 1968 paper changed the course of
economic theory. In just 17 pages, he demolished
existing theory and outlined an effective alternate
monetary policy designed to secure 'high employment,
stable prices and rapid growth.'

Friedman demonstrated that monetary policy plays
a vital role in broader economic stability and argued
that economists got their monetary policy wrong
in the 1950s and 1960s by misunderstanding the
relationship between inflation and unemployment.
Previous generations of economists had believed
that governments could permanently decrease
unemployment by permitting inflation—and vice versa.
Friedman's most original contribution was to show that
this supposed trade-off is an illusion that only works in
the short term.

Macat analyses are available from all good bookshops and libraries.

Access hundreds of analyses through one, multimedia tool.
Join free for one month **library.macat.com**

Macat Disciplines

Access the greatest ideas and thinkers across entire disciplines, including

THE FUTURE OF DEMOCRACY

Robert A. Dahl's, *Democracy and Its Critics*
Robert A. Dahl's, *Who Governs?*
Alexis De Toqueville's, *Democracy in America*
Niccolò Machiavelli's, *The Prince*
John Stuart Mill's, *On Liberty*
Robert D. Putnam's, *Bowling Alone*
Jean-Jacques Rousseau's, *The Social Contract*
Henry David Thoreau's, *Civil Disobedience*

Macat Pairs

Analyse historical and modern issues from opposite sides of an argument. Pairs include:

RACE AND IDENTITY

Zora Neale Hurston's
Characteristics of Negro Expression

Using material collected on anthropological expeditions to the South, Zora Neale Hurston explains how expression in African American culture in the early twentieth century departs from the art of white America. At the time, African American art was often criticized for copying white culture. For Hurston, this criticism misunderstood how art works. European tradition views art as something fixed. But Hurston describes a creative process that is alive, ever-changing, and largely improvisational. She maintains that African American art works through a process called 'mimicry'—where an imitated object or verbal pattern, for example, is reshaped and altered until it becomes something new, novel—and worthy of attention.

Frantz Fanon's
Black Skin, White Masks

Black Skin, White Masks offers a radical analysis of the psychological effects of colonization on the colonized.

Fanon witnessed the effects of colonization first hand both in his birthplace, Martinique, and again later in life when he worked as a psychiatrist in another French colony, Algeria. His text is uncompromising in form and argument. He dissects the dehumanizing effects of colonialism, arguing that it destroys the native sense of identity, forcing people to adapt to an alien set of values—including a core belief that they are inferior. This results in deep psychological trauma.

Fanon's work played a pivotal role in the civil rights movements of the 1960s.

Macat analyses are available from all good bookshops and libraries.

Access hundreds of analyses through one, multimedia tool.
Join free for one month **library.macat.com**

Macat Pairs

Analyse historical and modern issues from opposite sides of an argument. Pairs include:

INTERNATIONAL RELATIONS IN THE 21ˢᵀ CENTURY

Samuel P. Huntington's
The Clash of Civilisations

In his highly influential 1996 book, Huntington offers a vision of a post-Cold War world in which conflict takes place not between competing ideologies but between cultures. The worst clash, he argues, will be between the Islamic world and the West: the West's arrogance and belief that its culture is a "gift" to the world will come into conflict with Islam's obstinacy and concern that its culture is under attack from a morally decadent "other."

Clash inspired much debate between different political schools of thought. But its greatest impact came in helping define American foreign policy in the wake of the 2001 terrorist attacks in New York and Washington.

Francis Fukuyama's
The End of History and the Last Man

Published in 1992, *The End of History and the Last Man* argues that capitalist democracy is the final destination for all societies. Fukuyama believed democracy triumphed during the Cold War because it lacks the "fundamental contradictions" inherent in communism and satisfies our yearning for freedom and equality. Democracy therefore marks the endpoint in the evolution of ideology, and so the "end of history." There will still be "events," but no fundamental change in ideology.

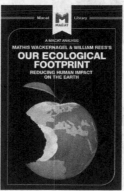

Macat Pairs

Analyse historical and modern issues
from opposite sides of an argument.
Pairs include:

ARE WE FUNDAMENTALLY GOOD - OR BAD?

Steven Pinker's
The Better Angels of Our Nature

Stephen Pinker's gloriously optimistic 2011 book argues that, despite humanity's biological tendency toward violence, we are, in fact, less violent today than ever before. To prove his case, Pinker lays out pages of detailed statistical evidence. For him, much of the credit for the decline goes to the eighteenth-century Enlightenment movement, whose ideas of liberty, tolerance, and respect for the value of human life filtered down through society and affected how people thought. That psychological change led to behavioral change—and overall we became more peaceful. Critics countered that humanity could never overcome the biological urge toward violence; others argued that Pinker's statistics were flawed.

Philip Zimbardo's
The Lucifer Effect

Some psychologists believe those who commit cruelty are innately evil. Zimbardo disagrees. In *The Lucifer Effect*, he argues that sometimes good people do evil things simply because of the situations they find themselves in, citing many historical examples to illustrate his point. Zimbardo details his 1971 Stanford prison experiment, where ordinary volunteers playing guards in a mock prison rapidly became abusive. But he also describes the tortures committed by US army personnel in Iraq's Abu Ghraib prison in 2003—and how he himself testified in defence of one of those guards. committed by US army personnel in Iraq's Abu Ghraib prison in 2003—and how he himself testified in defence of one of those guards.

Macat Pairs

Analyse historical and modern issues from opposite sides of an argument. Pairs include:

HOW WE RELATE TO EACH OTHER AND SOCIETY

Jean-Jacques Rousseau's
The Social Contract

Rousseau's famous work sets out the radical concept of the 'social contract': a give-and-take relationship between individual freedom and social order.

If people are free to do as they like, governed only by their own sense of justice, they are also vulnerable to chaos and violence. To avoid this, Rousseau proposes, they should agree to give up some freedom to benefit from the protection of social and political organization. But this deal is only just if societies are led by the collective needs and desires of the people, and able to control the private interests of individuals. For Rousseau, the only legitimate form of government is rule by the people.

Robert D. Putnam's
Bowling Alone

In *Bowling Alone*, Robert Putnam argues that Americans have become disconnected from one another and from the institutions of their common life, and investigates the consequences of this change.

Looking at a range of indicators, from membership in formal organizations to the number of invitations being extended to informal dinner parties, Putnam demonstrates that Americans are interacting less and creating less "social capital" – with potentially disastrous implications for their society.

It would be difficult to overstate the impact of *Bowling Alone*, one of the most frequently cited social science publications of the last half-century.

Printed in the United States
by Baker & Taylor Publisher Services